A Santali Grammar For Beginners

A Santali Grammar For Beginners

By

The Rev. P. O. Bodding

GYAN

Published by

GYAN

Gyan Publishing House
5, Ansari Road
Daryaganj, New Delhi-110002
Phone: 011-47034999, 9811692060
E-mail: books@gyanbooks.com

Distribution Network
gyanbooks.com
India, USA, Canada, UK, Australia, France

ISBN : 978-81-212-6731-1 (PB)
First Published, 1929

2nd Impression 2022

Printed at: Gyan Press, Delhi.

A SANTALI GRAMMAR FOR BEGINNERS
Author: THE REV. P. O. BODDING

A
SANTALI GRAMMAR
FOR
BEGINNERS

BY

The Rev. P. O. Bodding

1929

Preface.

Quite a number of people are studying the Santali language; and as at present no short grammar for the use of beginners is to be had, the writer was prevailed upon to give a sketch of the language. The result is what is found in the following pages.

Any one who wishes to enter more fully on the study of the language may be referred to the author's Materials for a Santali Grammar, I and II to be had from the Mission Press at Benagaria. Part I that principally deals with the phonetics of the language is at present out of print, but a new edition will, I trust, be available before long.

Mohulpahari,
Santal Parganas } 19th April 1929.

P. O. Bodding

The Santali Letters.

I. In writing or printing Santali the following characters are used :

Vowels : *a, e̱, e, i, o̱, o, u.*

,, (resultant) : *ạ, ẹ, ọ,*

,, (nasalized) : *ã, ạ̃, ẽ̱, ẽ, ĩ, õ̱, õ, ũ.*

Of these the following diphthong combinations are used :-

ae, ao, ạiׅ, ạu, ea, eo, e̱o̱, e̱o, iạ, io, iu, oa, oe, o̱e, o̱i, uạ, ui.

which may all be nasalized ; the sign of nasalization is for the sake of convenience ordinarily put only on the first part of the diphthong, although, of course, the whole combination partakes of the nasalization.

Consonants :								
Glottal :	*h.*							
Velar (guttural) :	*k,*	*kh,*	*g,*	*gh,*	*ṅ,*			*k'*
Palatal :	*c,*	*ch,*	*j,*	*jh,*	*ń,*	*y,*		*c'*
Cacuminal (cerebral) :	*ṭ,*	*ṭh,*	*ḍ,*	*ḍh,*	*ṇ,*	*ṛ,*		
Dental :	*t,*	*th,*	*d,*	*dh,*	*n,*	*r,*	*l,*	*t'*
Labial :	*p,*	*ph,*	*b,*	*bh,*	*m,*	*v.*	*w,*	*p'*
Sibilant :	*s.*							

The Roman alphabet is used with the addition of diacritical marks where necessary.

2. The diacritical marks used are as follows :

With *vowels* :

a *circumflex* above a vowel (as in *ã*) to show nasalization of the vowel sound ;

a *dash* below a vowel to show the open vowel sound, as against the closed (used with e̠ and o̠ only);

a *dot* below a vowel (as in ạ) to show that the vowel is of the kind which is now called *resultant*.

With *consonants*:

a *dot* below to show that the consonant stands for a cacuminal (cerebral) sound (as with ṭ);

an *accent* (acc. aigu) to show that the consonant is a palatal (used only with ń);

a *point* above to show that the consonant is velar or guttural (only with ṅ);

an *apostrophe* above or on the right top side to show that the character is a checked consonant (*k'*, *c'*, *t'*, *p'*).

3. As regards the pronunciation of the vowels the following should be noted:

a is pronounced something like the *a* in *father*;

ạ is a sound peculiar to Santali. To an untrained ear it sounds like something between the vowels in *hut* and *hat*. Scandinavians should avoid pronouncing it like ö.

e is like the *e* in Norw. *se*, Germ. *See*, and also in Engl. *met*.

e̠ is like the vowel in Engl. *fair* and *fat*.

i like in Engl. *pit* or *police*.

o like in Norw. *stor* and *sort*, Engl. *low*.

o̠ like the vowel in Engl. *law*, *all*, *hot*.

ǫ a sound peculiar to Santali, necessary to differentiate words like *kol,* to send, *kǫl,* machinery, and *kǫl*, the Indian cuckoo.

u like the vowel in French *tour*, Norw. *sur, hus*, Engl. *rude, put.*

All vowels may be long or short; all may be nasalized.

As regards the diphthongs, they may be descending (with stress on the first vowel), ascending (with stress on the second vowel), or level (with equal tone-length on both vowels). Santali diphthongs consist of two vowels, not of a vowel and a semiconsonant.

4. As regards the consonants: Pronunciation is about the same as of the same characters in transliterated Hindi.

Where no diacritical marks are used the pronunciation is with certain reservations the same as in English.

All consonants are either unaspirated or fully aspirated, not like in many European languages slightly aspirated. All aspirated consonants are shown by an *h* added (*kh, gh, ch, etc.*).

An aspirated consonant is pronounced by superimposing the glottal (*h*) on the off-glide of the stopped consonant.

The Dentals are pure dentals, not supradentals or alveolars like in English, that is to say, in pronunciation of a dental the tip of the tongue touches the back of the teeth, not the alveoli.

5. The following should be noted in connection with the consonants :

g has always the hard sound, like in *gape*.

c is always palatal, pronounced like the Italian *c* before *i*, and somewhat like Engl. *ch* in *church*.

j is palatal, pronounced somewhat like Engl. *j* in *jack* or *g* in *gentle*.

y is never a vowel, but a semiconsonant, pronounced somewhat like *j* in Danish *ja* or *reje*. It is not initial in ordinary Santali and is mostly used euphonically to avoid hiatus.

v and *w* are pronounced like in English. Not initial; *w* is often used euphonically like *y*.

ṭ, *ṭh*, *ḍ*, *ḍh*, *ṇ*, *ṛ*, the so-called cerebral sounds are all pronounced with the tip of the tongue retroflexed. When pronouncing the first five the underside of the tip of the tongue touches the palate just behind the alveoli; *ṇ* is rarely heard, except before a *ṭ* or a *ḍ*.

ṛ, a sound that gives many Europeans trouble, is pronounced by drawing the inverted tip of the tongue up towards the middle of the hard palate, but without touching the palate. The tip of the tongue is then moved rapidly forward towards the front teeth along the palate, which, however, is not touched. When passing the upper gum the inverted tongue tip momentarily touches this. The end of the movement is that the tongue tip strikes against the lower front teeth, at the same time doing away with the inversion. It is a rough kind of sound and not difficult to one knowing how to produce it.

r is pronounced by vibrating the tip of the tongue; it is different from the English 'vowel' *r*, more like the Scotch *r*, very much the same as the sound heard in the south-eastern parts of Norway.

l is the same sound as heard in Norw. or Danish.

ṅ is the guttural nasal, pronounced like *ng* in Engl. *song*.

ń is the palatal nasal, pronounced like the *gn* in the French *agneau* or the Spanish *ñ* in *señor*. It is somewhat different from the Engl. initial sounds in words like *new*.

6. Besides the sounds mentioned Santali has four checked consonants, written with an apostrophe above or at the right hand top of the consonant in question. There is one guttural (*k'*), one palatal (*c'*), one dental (*t'*) and one labial (*p'*) checked consonant.

The consonant is formed in the mouth, but has no off-glide, or in other words, the consonant in question (always voiceless) is articulated, the air passage is momentarily closed at a particular point and then suddenly opened for, when the stop is released and the tongue or lip-position is so altered as to let nothing more be heard of the consonant or its off-glide.

7. In connection with pronunciation the)following should be noted: The vowels of adjoining syllables influence each other; open and closed vowels will not easily go together. When an *a* or an *o* has an *i* or an *u* in the adjoining syllable of the same stress-unit (or there has been such a one, but is lost in the present language), the *a* or *o* becomes resultant (*ạ* or *ọ*). An *a* and *i* or *u* (*ai*, *au*)

cannot go together in a diphthong. The same happens, when other vowels occur in syllables adjoining an *i* or *u*; but as these resultant vowels are less easily distinguishable, they are generally not written.

A resultant vowel is, however, also often changed into an ordinary vowel that will go with *i* or *u*. The rules of the laws of Harmonic Sequence will be found in Mat. I., paras 19 ss. *

8. The intonation of Santali (the melody of the language, if one likes) is fairly level, rising and falling inside the sentence; but the language has no 'tones' (like what is found in e. g. Chinese), and no compound or dissyllabic intonation (such as heard, e. g., in the western parts of Norway or in Swedish). Stress is also fairly equal on the syllables, stress depending more on vowel quantity or length than on anything else.

9. All words have either initial vowel or initial single consonant; inside a word combinations of two consonants are frequent, sometimes of even three, but then one of these is a nasal.

10. The Santal language is agglutinative. What in inflexional languages is done by declination, etc., is here brought about by the addition of suffixes and postpositions. The word itself is left untouched.

11. Practically all words may function as nouns, adjectives, verbs and adverbs, without any alteration in form. For the sake of convenience we shall here deal

---

* The reader who wants further information is referred to the author's Materials for a Santali Grammar, I and II, here quoted as Mat. I. and Mat. II. both to be had from the Mission Press, Benagaria.

with the words functioning as the one or the other; but it should be remembered that the words are not exclusively nouns, or adjectives, etc., but function as such.

Naturally many words have by use or on account of meaning been restricted to function as only nouns, etc.; but there is nothing to hinder any word from taking a verbal suffix; even a pronoun or an interjection may be used as a verb.

Before commencing to deal with the different parts of speech, something has to be said concerning Gender, Number and Determinative Suffixes.

Gender.

12. Except in words borrowed from Aryan languages Santali does not *formally* distinguish between genders. The language has a large number of borrowed words representing the male and the female ending respectively in *a* and *i*.

Koṛa, a boy; *kuṛi*, a girl.
Kala, deaf (m.); *kạli*, deaf (f.).
Leḍha, limping (m.); *liḍhi*, limping (f.).
Bheḍa, a ram: *bhiḍi*, a sheep.

But

Hoṛ, man, Santal (m. and f.).
Usul, high, tall (both m. and f.).
Nanha, thin (m. and f.).
Huḍiń, small (m. and f.).
Keṭec', strong (m. and f.).

13. While the language does not formally, except as stated, distinguish genders, it distinguishes between

the sexes, where such exist and are observable, (a) by using separate words, or (b) by prefixing or adding a word showing the sex to another word denoting the common gender.

(a) *Hęrẹl*, man, male; *maejiu*, woman.
Aṇḍia, male; *eṅga*, mother, female.
Haṛam, an old man; *buḍhi*, an old woman.
Ḍaṅgra, bullock; *gại*, cow.
Kaḍa, a buffalo (m.); *bitkil*, a buffalo cow.

(b) *Seta*, dog; *ạṇḍiạ seta*, a male dog; *eṅga seta*, a bitch.
Pusi, cat; *pusi ạṇḍiạ*, a male cat; *pusi eṅga*, a female cat.
Sim, fowl; *sim sạṇḍi*, a cock; *sim eṅga*, a hen.

14. The language distinguishes between the *animate* and the *inanimate*, and this distinction to a large degree affects the grammatical construction of the whole language.

The distinction is not between living and dead, or between spirit or matter, but between what, according to Santal ideas, has a soul and what has not. The animate is matter with a living force inside that makes it capable of acting and moving.

A living tres is inanimate, so is *jivi* (soul) and *jiu* (spirit).

As animate the Santals consider: all living beings, also fishes and insects; the sun, moon and stars; God; the bongas and other spirits; also the ancestors; anything representing a living being, such as figures. Even when dead, beings are treated grammatically as animate, provided the same name is used.

The demonstrative, interrogative and indefinite pronouns have different forms for the animate and the inanimate. The same is the case with certain suffixes. In the verb the inanimate subject and object are not shown, with certain exceptions that will be mentioned further on.

Number.

15. The language has three numbers, the Singular, the Dual and the Plural.

The Singular is the bare word ; the Dual is formed by adding *kin*, and the Plural by adding *ko* to the Singular. *Kin* and *ko* will be found again under the Personal pronouns.

Animates and inanimates form the Dual and the Plural in the same way. If the number is otherwise shown, the *kin* and the *ko* are often left out ; if used in such cases, they often convey the same meaning as a definite article.

Inanimates do not take number suffixes, except when absolutely needed to show number.

Sadom, a horse ; *sadomkin*, two horses ; *sadomko*, horses (more than two).
Orak, a house ; *orakkin*, two houses ; *orakko*, houses.
Bar hor, two persons ; *ponea gai*, four cows.
Pe orak, three houses.

16. The Plural suffix is often added to express the indefinite, the class, one of a number of possibilities. It is also constantly added, when a number of words are enumerated, also names of things that otherwise never take a plural suffix.

Nawa perako hec'ena, new friends have arrived (about the birth of a child).

Hoṛko, Dekoko, Musl̥ako, Santals, Hindus, Muhammedans.

Hoṛoko, joṇḍrako, gundliko, paddy, Indian corn, millet.

In connection with numbers the following should be noted: Parents-in-law and children-in-law address each other and speak of themselves in conversation with each other, always using the Dual, when meaning only one. The other party is mentally included.

People whose children have married use, addressing each other and speaking of themselves in conversation, the Plural.

Determinative Suffixes.

17. Santali makes use of certain determinative suffixes, different for animates and inanimates.

For animates this is in the Singular *-ic'*, in the Dual and the Plural respectively *-kin* and *-ko*.

The inanimate determinative suffix is in the Singular *-ak'*, with *-ak'kin* and *-ak'ko* in the Dual and the Plural. In stead of *ak' aṅ* is also used.

These suffixes are used to single out, to show the concretely existing. They often do service for our determined article.

Goc'ic', the dead one; *dadalic'*, the one who beats (did the beating); *dal ocoyenic'*, the one who was beaten; *bogeyic'*, the good one; *baṛic'ic'*, the bad one; *kiriṅak'ko*, the things bought; *seawak'*, what is rotten.

These suffixes are often used to form possessive adjectives, doing service for our genitive. *Aleyic̆*, our one; *amic̆ koṛa*, your boy; *amak' oṛak'*, your house.

Nouns.

18. Most words may in Santali function as nouns; but there is nothing in the words themselves formally to show that they are nouns.

Number is shown, when needed, by adding a number suffix. See para 15.

There is nothing to show formally the gender (except, as previously mentioned, in borrowed words) or the animate or the inanimate. See paras 12-14.

19. There is no declension of nouns; the base-word is not altered; what in other languages is effected through declension is in Santali attained by the use of postpositions of sorts (the language does not use prepositions). See below paras 21—33. *Hoṛ*, a man, a Santal; *jel*, a dear (animate), meat, flesh (inanimate); *hoṛ*, a road; *jom*, food, eat; *kombṛo*, thief (animate), theft (inanimate); *raj*, king, zemindar (animate), kingdom, zemindary (inanimate).

The Article.

20. The numeral *mit'*, one, is made to serve as an indefinite article, either in this bare form or with *ṭen*, *ṭeč* or *ṭaṅ*, or *goṭen*, *goṭeč* or *goṭaṅ* added.

To express our definite article the language makes use of the demonstrative pronouns or the determinative suffixes.

The real meaning of the numeral and the demonstrative is probably never quite lost; a word without any prefix of the kind mentioned may have to be translated, according to need, with a word with an indefinite or a definite article.

Mit' hor̥, one man, a man; *mit'ten sadom*, a horse; *mit'tec' dare*, a tree; *mit' guten hor*, a man; *uni kora*, the boy, that boy; *koraic'*, the boy; *dokan menak'a*, there is a shop; *dokanteye calaoena*, he went to the shop.

The Postpositions.

21. As remarked the language has no declension corresponding to what is found in the inflexional languages. In stead of declension and also to do service for prepositions the language makes use of a large number of postpositions, the most common ones of which will be shown here below.

The postpositions may be added to nouns, adjectives and words with verbal suffixes (not, however, when functioning as finite verbs, or in the Imperative).

Most of the postpositions may, when functioning, take the determinative suffixes and the suffixed personal pronouns.

22. Postpositions showing *rest in:*

rẹ * means in, inside, within, within the boundaries of the concept of the word to which it is added. It is used about space, time, action or relation. It may be translated *in, on, at, during, while, in —case*, or with similar words.

* To show the pronunciation the open vowels have been partly shown in this section; ordinarily they are not written (not *rẹ*, etc., but *re, ren, then, te, sen, khon*). The pronunciation of the ẹ varies in acc. with the laws of Harmonic Sequence.

Oṛak̕re, in the house; *birre*, in the forest; *o̱tre*, on the ground; *ho̱ere*, in the air; *co̱ṭre*, high up; *latarre*, down below; *jo̱khe̱c' re*, at the time; *tinre*, at what time (during the day); *cando hạsurok̕re*, at sunset; *e̱nḍe̱re*, then, in that case. *Re* may be said to correspond to a Locative.

23. *Re̱n* is *re̱* with the adjective forming *n* added and conveys the meaning of somebody being inside of, belonging to what the word referred to stands for. The word referred to is animate.

Oṛak̕ren, who is in, belongs to the house; *dak̕ren hako*, fish in the water; *ac'ren koṛa*, his own boy; *birren janwar*, a forest animal; *amren gại*, your cow.

In practical use it generally does service corresponding to our Genitive.

24. *Reak̕* (or *reaṅ*) is *re* with the inanimate determinative suffix added; used like *ren* and with the same meaning, but only referring to inanimates.

Oṛak̕ reak̕ sạṛim, the roof of the house; *dak̕' reak̕' khạndrite̱t'*, the depth of the water; *bir reak̕ dare*, a tree from the forest; *hapṛamko reak̕ katha*, the story of the ancestors, the traditions; *am reaṅko ro̱ṛe̱ta*, they are talking of you.

Note the compound postpositions *talare*, among, between, in the middle of; *modre*, *mudre*, *mo̱to̱re*, among (not between).

25. To express *rest with*:

Ṭhe̱n or *ṭhe̱c'* is used. While *re* is *in*, *ṭhe̱n* is *at*, *with*. It is used about space and about immaterial relation.

Oṛak' ṭhe̱n, at the house (not in, but close by outside); *apat ṭhe̱n*, with his father; *dhiri ṭhe̱n*, at the stone (not on); *mit' ṭhe̱n*, at one place; *guru ṭhe̱n kulijoṅme*, ask (with) the teacher; *hạkim ṭhe̱n e̱ktiạri menak̕'a*, the hakim has authority (is with).

26. Postpositions denoting *movement towards.*

Ṭhen or *ṭhec'* is used to denote movement towards an animate being, and also to anything inanimate, when a movement up to is intended : *to, up to.*

Apuń ṭheniń calak'a, I shall go to my father; *hakim ṭhen kathako aderket'a,* they brought the matter in before the magistrate; *culha ṭhec' dohoeme,* put it just beside the fireplace.

Te is used to denote movement towards, or direction to or along, but only to inanimates; it may also mean into : *to, into, along.*

Oṛak'teye calaoena, he went home; *okatem calak' kana,* where are you going? *birte,* to the forest; *hor horte,* along the road; *otteko calaoena,* they went walking.

Sen or *sec'* means *towards, in the direction of, on the side of, in favour of.*

Ato senko rakap'ena, they went up towards the village; *dak' sec',* towards water; *coṭ sec' beṅgedme,* look upwards; *onko sec',* in their direction, in their favour.

Dhabic', (with parallel forms *dharic', habic'* and *haric'*) means *up to, unto, until.* Used about space and time and also figuratively.

Sako dhabic', up to the bridge; *mucat' habic',* until the end; *Kolkata dhabic',* to Calcutta (not further); *tis dhabic',* up to when; *teheń haric',* until to day; *hatlak' dhabic',* up to the armpit; *gel ṭaka dhabic',* up to ten rupees (not more); *gujuk' habic',* until death.

27. Postposition to denote *movement from.*

Khon (or *khoc'*) is used to denote movement *from,* and also separation from, origin from, distinguishing from. It is used about space and time, and also source. It is the opposite of *dhabic'.*

Bhitri khon, from inside ; *khet khon,* from the rice-field ; *Dumka khon,* from Dumka ; *gapa khon mean dhabic',* from to-morrow until the day after; *etohop' khon mucat' habic',* from beginning to end.

28. Postpositions to denote *association with.*

Tuluc' denotes being *with,* association with, meeting with.

Am tuluc'e hec'lena, he came with you ; *mohajon tuluc'e gatek' kana,* he is keeping on friendly terms with the money-lender ; *puthi tuluc' selet aguime,* bring the slate together with the book ; *raj tuluc'ko laṛhaiyena,* they fought their landlord.

Selet' denotes addition to, company *with.*

Apat selet'ko hec'ena, they came together with their father ; *hopon selet' eṅgattet',* the mother with her young ones.

Salak', together with (used like *selet').*

Sāo (to which *re* or *te* is frequently added), *together with.*

Sagaṛ sāote, along with the cart ; *hoṛ sāore,* together with people.

Lagae (*te*), is used to denote inclusion with, *in conjunction with.* The person or thing included is always an integral part of the 'company'.

Mañjhi lagaete, in conjunction with the village headman ; *nesak' lagaete,* with this year's added.

29. Postpositions to express *instrumentality, cause* and *means.*

Then (*thec'*) is used to show the one through or by whom something happens, also often the agent of the Passive. In this meaning only used added to animates.

Ojha then, by the ojha ; *guti koṛa thene lajao ocoyena,* he was put to shame by the servant ; *kaḍa thene rok'ena,* he was gored by a buffalo.

Tẹ is used to denote the instrument or the means by or with which anything is done or accomplished, also the price (buying or selling) and the cause. *By, through, with, for, on account of.*

Tẹṅgọc'teye mak'kedea, he cut him with an axe; *tite,* with the hand; *họete bindaṛena,* it was brought down by the wind; *ac'te,* by himself, of his own accord; *cet' lekate,* how, in what way; *sadọmte,* by horse (riding); *bọtọrte,* from fear; *raskạte,* with joy; *pon anate,* for four annas; *utińte,* by barter.

Note the frequent use of *te* added to a noun with *kin* or *ko* added to denote a pair or a company. *Apatteko,* the father and those with him; *kakańteko,* my uncle and his ones.

This *te* is very frequently added to another word forming a compound postposition.

Iạte, on account of, because. *Ruạ iạte,* because of fever.

Họtẹtẹ, by, through (generally added to animates; frequently used to show the agent of the Passive). *Am họtẹte,* because of you (being present); *dak' họtẹte,* on account of rain (then falling).

Hũyạ̃te, because of. *Apat hũyạ̃te,* because of his father.

30. Postpositions to show *purpose, intention, designation* and *benefit.*

Lạgit' (or *lagat'*), for the purpose of, for.

Am lạgit', for you; *ran lạgit',* for the purpose of medicine; *noa ciṭhi dọ ọkọe lạgit'?* for whom is this letter? *kol lạgit',* in order to send.

Ńutumte, in the name of, for the sake of.

Mante, *marte* and *mente* are other postpositions constantly used to show the purpose, or also the manner or mode.

31. *Kate* is a postposition, mostly used as a verbal suffix, signifying *by doing, having done*; it is also used in connection with distributives.

Onakate, thereafter; *senkate*, having gone; *durup'-kate*, sitting down; *barea kate*, in twos, each two.

Kate is also frequently used as a conjunction at the commencement of a sentence in the meaning of thereupon, after this.

32. Two other postpositions of very frequent occurrence are *ante* and *ate*; like *kate* they really belong to the verb. *Ante* means having, or with, *ate* signifies the accompanying circumstances, with.

Horante, with people, having people with oneself; *ak' sar ante*, with bow and arrow; *serenate*, singing; *ruate*, with drumming; *horate*, accompanied by people.

33. If we compare the Santali use of postpositions with the declension of an inflexional language, we will get something like the following:

Nominative:	no postposition.
Genitive:	*ren* (when the following word is animate). *ak'*, *an*, *reak'*, *rean* (when the word referred to is inanimate).
Dative:	*then* (*thec'*), *lagit'* (*lagat'*), *nutumte*, *te*.
Accusative:	no postposition.
Instrumental:	*then*, *te*, *hotete*.
Ablative:	*khon*.
Locative:	*re*, *te*, *dhabic'*, *then*.
Vocative:	no postposition, but an interjection (*E*, *henda*, etc. prefixed, or *ho* added).

There is no difference in postpositions added to the singular, the dual and the plural.

Examples :

Nominative :	*haṛam*, the old man.
Genitive :	*haṛamren* (e. g. *koṛa*), the old man's (e. g. boy).
„	*haṛamak'* (e. g. *kicric'*), the old man's (e. g. cloth). (or *haṛam reak'*, - *reaṅ*, -*aṅ*)
Dative :	*haṛam ṭhen*, to the old man ; *haṛam lạgit'*, for the old man ; *haṛam ńutumte*, for the old man('s sake).
Accusative :	*haṛam*, the old man.
Instrumental :	*haṛam ṭhen*, with, by the old man ; *haṛam hoṭẹte*, through the old man.
Ablative :	*haṛam khon*, from the old man.
Locative :	*haṛamre*, in the old man, on do. ; *haṛam dhạbic'*, up to, until the old man ; *haṛam ṭhen*, with, at the old man.
Vocative :	*E haṛam*, O old man (*henda haṛam*, do.).

Nominative :	*bir*, forest.
Genitive :	*birren* (e. g. *janwar*), (an animal) of the forest. *birak'* (- *aṅ*, *reak'*, *reaṅ*) (e. g. *dare*), (a tree) of the forest.
Dative :	*bir lạgit'*, for the forest ; *bir ńutumte*, for the (sake of the) forest ; *birte*, to the forest.
Accusative :	*bir*, the forest.
Instrumental :	*birte*, through the forest ; *ṭheṅgate*, with a stick.
Ablative :	*bir khon*, from the forest.
Locative :	*birre*, in the forest ; *birte*, to the forest, *bir dhạbic'*, up to the forest ; *bir ṭhen*, at the forest.

Note : the language has no cases ; above is put down as a help to those whose mother tongue is inflexional.

The Adjectives.

34. Any word may function as an adjective; two or more words may be placed side by side, one acting as the noun, the other or others as adjectives. As a rule, but not necessarily the word functioning as an adjective precedes the noun.

Words functioning as adjectives are subject to the same laws as when serving as nouns, as to number, gender and lack of declension.

Except in borrowed words there is no special form to show gender; the same word may be used for the animate and the inanimate.

Words with a determinative suffix, with a verbal suffix, or even a whole sentence, or with a postposition may function as an adjective.

Boge hoṛ, a good man; *boge caole*, good rice; *bogeyic'* the good one; *bogeak'*, what is good; *bogeko*, the good ones; *kala hoṛ*, a deaf man; *kali hoṛ*, a deaf person (female); *bir dare*, a forest tree; *oṛak' hoṛ*, a house person (i. e. husband or wife); *hoṛ oṛak'*, a Santal house; *calaoen hapta*, last week; *hijuk' cando*, coming month.

35. All words having final single vowel may in Santali get an *n* added; the word thus formed may function as an adjective and frequently so does.

Above mentioned postposition *ren* is *re* + this *n*. The same *n* is constantly met with after the demonstrative adverbs, such as *onḍen*, who, what is there, *nonkan*, who, what is like this, *lekan*, like. Also common with other words, such as *teṅgon*, standing, *edren*, angry, *tahen*, remaining, staying, *eton*, fit for being broken in.

Degrees of comparison.

36. Comparative is expressed by putting the post-position *khon* after the word with which comparison is to be made and leaving the other word as it is.

It may also be effected by putting *bạṛti* (more), *ar*, *arhõ*, *artẹt'* (more, still more, additional) before the adjective, with a word with or without *khon* after the compared word.

Am khon maraṅ, bigger than you; *iñ khon daṛe-aniċ'*, stronger than myself; *hana dare khon noa dọ usul*, this tree is higher than that one; *bạṛti sebel*, more savoury; *artẹt' kisạ̃ṛ*, still more wealthy.

Superlative may be expressed by putting *jọtọ* or *sanam* (all) followed by *khon* and compare with this. *Jọtọ khon maraṅ*, biggest of all.

Or *utạr* (the utmost) may be added to the adjective. *Cọṭ utạr*, the highest; *boge utạr*, the best.

The Numerals.

The Cardinal Numerals.

37. The Santals have the following numbers:

1. *mit'*.
2. *bar* (or *barea*).
3. *pẹ* (or *pea*).
4. *pon* (or *ponea*).
5. *mõṛẽ*.
6. *turui*.
7. *eae*.
8. *irạl*.
9. *arẹ* (*are*)
10. *gẹl*.
11. *gẹl mit'*.
12. *gẹl bar* (- *barea*).

13. *gel pe (- pea).*
14. *gel pon (- ponea).*
15. *gel mõrẽ.*
16. *gel turui.*
17. *gel eae.*
18. *gel iral.*
19. *gel are.*
20. *mit' isi* or *bar gel.*
21. *mit' isi mit'* or *bar gel mit'.*
22. *mit' isi bar* or *bar gel bar.*
30. *mit' isi gel* or *pe gel.*
40. *bar isi* or *pon gel.*
50. *bar isi gel* or *mõrẽ gel.*
60. *pe isi* or *turui gel.*
70. *pe isi gel* or *eae gel.*
80. *pon isi* or *iral gel.*
90. *pon isi gel* or *are gel.*
100. *mit' sae* or *mõrẽ isi.*
123. *turui isi pea* or *mit' sae bar gel pe.*
1000. *mit' hajar.*
100,000. *mit' lak.*

38. The Santals count up to ten and then add the units, often with a *khon* between (e. g. *gel khon barea,* from ten two, i. e., twelve), up to twenty. Higher numbers are multiples of twenties or tens, adding the units. Now-a days the Bengali or Hindi numerals are very commonly used.

39. In connection with counting the following words should be noted : *ganda,* a quadruplet, is very commonly used as a unit in counting. Five *ganda* make one *kuri,* or one *isi,* or one *bis* (other names for a score). Four *isi* make one *pon* (eighty), used in counting paddy seedlings and straw bundles and certain other things (cocoons, Indian corn cobs, etc.).

Adha, half, *tala* or *tara,* half ; *pawa* or *poa,* a quart.

Mõṛẽ gaṇḍa kāṛã kạuḍi dọ mit' poesa, five fours of shells make one pice; *mit' isi gaṇḍa joṇḍra phọṭ dọ mit' pọn,* one score fours of Indian corn cobs is eighty: *adha disom* half the country; *tala sẹr,* half a seer; *tala moka,* half a cubit; *bar poesa tala,* two and a half pice; *mit' din tala,* one and a half day.

40. To render fractions, besides the words mentioned (*adha, tala, pawa*), the language has no special words; one has to make use of descriptive combinations, such as *pẹ hạṭińre bar hạṭiń,* two thirds, *gẹl hạṭińre mit' hạṭiń,* one tenth.

Distributive Numerals.

41. Distributive numerals are formed of the first ten numerals by reduplicating the first consonant and following vowel, and (when the numeral has initial vowel) by inserting an *-k'* after the first vowel:

mimit', each one, one by one.
babar, each two.
pẹpẹ, each three.
popon, each four.
mõmõṛ, each five.
tutur, each six.
ek'eae, each seven.
ik'ral, each eight.
ak're, each nine.
gẹgẹl, each ten.
babar isi, each forty, etc.

The distributives require something added; this may be a word showing what is distributed, or it may be *goṭań, gọṭẹc'* or *gọṭẹn* (piece). Frequently *kate* is added either to the distributive numeral or to the words just mentioned.

Mimit' phuṛuk' emakope, give them each one leaf-cup; *dinre popon ana kateko ńama*, they get four annas each daily; *pẹpẹ gọṭẹc' kateko hẹc'ena*, they came in parties of three. *Mimit' mimit' hoṛ*, one by one, one by one person, i. e. some people, one here one there; *mimit' mimit'te*, one by one, the one after the other, each one.

The Ordinal Numerals.

42. Santali has properly speaking only three ordinal numerals, all borrowed from Hindi, viz., *pạhil*, *dosar* (*dosra*) and *tesar* (*tesra*), first, second and third. *Cạuṭha*, fourth, is getting into use. All are used about both animates and inanimates.

The lack of ordinals is due to the little need of such in the daily life of the people. When in need of such they manage in several ways. Inside the family they use *maraṅ*, *tala* and *huḍiń* (lit. big, middle and little) for the first, second and third (son, etc.); when more, they use *sạńjhlạ* (or for girls *sạńjhli*) about the third, and *mạńjhlạ* (or *mạńjhli*) about the fourth; further *maraṅ tala* (big middle), *huḍiń tala* (small middle), and so on.

Frequently they do not refer to the position inside the whole, but to the relative position of two. In such cases *sotok'*, following, or *tayọm* (*taenọm*), after, behind, are commonly used. *Pạṇḍu sotok'*, the one who comes after P. in age; *turui tayọmic'*, the one after six, the seventh.

When the determinative suffix singular is added to a numeral, the expression is understood as being equal to an ordinal number. *Pẹ gẹl mit'ak'*, the thirty first;

areyic', the ninth; *gelak' hatiń*, the tenth part (one tenth).

43. The language has three collective or inclusive numerals, formed from the second, third and fourth numeral by infixing an *n* after the vowel which is repeated, viz., *banar*, both, *pene*, all three, and *ponon*, all four.

Banar hor, both persons (*bana* is often used instead of *banar* in combination with *hor*, otherwise not); *dene banar sec'renko*, the persons of both sides; *pene mĩhũń akriṅket'koa*, I sold all three calves; *ponon gidrako ruak' kana*, all four children are suffering from fever.

44. An aproximate number is expressed by naming two consecutive numbers, the lower numeral first; also by adding *leka* (something like), *gan* (about), or *leka gan*, or by prefixing *amdaj* (about).

Bar pe hor, two three persons, a couple; *mõrẽ turui*, five six; *mit' isi leka*, something like a score; *amdaj bar sae*, about two hundred; *amdaj pon isi leka gan hor*, something like about eighty people.

The Adverbs.

44. Bare words may function as adverbs, in this case frequently repeated, provided the meaning of the word lends itself to such use.

The language has a large number of words that are mostly used as adverbs, originally ordinary words.

By adding a postposition most words may function corresponding to our adverbs.

Pe sermae tahẽyena, he remained for three years; *nahake calaoena*, he went in vain; *bebaric'ko dalkedea*, they beat him terribly; *usarae hec'ena*, he came quickly;

purṭhaṅ beṅgeṭ'eṭ'a, I am seeing clearly; *koṛa koṛae ṅeloḱ kana,* he is looking like a young man; *thopa thopa jo akana,* it has fruited in clusters.

45. Some of the most common adverbially used words are given here below; some more will be found when we reach the demonstratives. The adverbs are conveniently divided into adverbs denoting *space, time, quantity, quality* and *manner.*

Words used adverbially denoting *place.*

Goṭa ṭaṇḍi, everywhere.	*Noa sa,* this side; *hana sa,* that side.
Laha, lahate, in front.	*Lahare,* in front.
Tayom, tayomte, behind, back.	*Tayomre,* behind (somewhere).
Samaṅ sec', towards the front.	*Samaṅre,* in front.
Latarte, downward.	*Latarre,* below, under.
Cetante, upwards.	*Cetanre,* above.
Coṭ, high up.	*Coṭre,* high up, on top.
Beṛhaete, round about.	*Beṛhae, beṛhaere, beṛhae sec',* round about.
Bahrete, outside.	*Bahre, bahrere, bahre sec',* outside.
Bhitrite, inside.	*Bhitri, bhitrire,* inside.
Aṛe aṛete, alongside.	*Aṛere,* on the side.

Otoṅ tayom, in file, one after the other (place, time, manner).

46. Words used adverbially denoting *time.*

Teheń, to day.	*Meaṅ,* the day after to-morrow.	*On mahnder,* three days ago.
Teheń gapa, at present.	*Endrae,* three days hence.	*Din kalom,* last year.
Nit, nitoḱ, now.		

Nãhãk̇ (*nahak̇*) now, at present, presently.
Nes, this year.
Netar, now-a-days.
Nebetar, now-a-days.
Siń, day, during day-time.
Ber, sun, day time.
Bela, sun, time of day.
Setak̇, morning, in the morning.
Jaoge, constantly.
Jaejuq, always.
Siń satup', all day long.
Mit' din, one day, some day.
Ursiń barsiń, a few days.
Bochor din, a year.
Pahilre, before.
Lahare, before.
Auri, later on, not yet.

Gapa, to-morrow.
Pher endrae, four days hence.
Kalom, next year.
Hola, yesterday.
Mahnder, the day before yesterday.
Satom, two years hence.
Ńinda, night, at night.
Ayup', evening, in the evening.
Sim rak̇, at cock-crow.
Jao hilok̇, daily.
Din hilok̇, every day.
Setak' piche, every morning.
Barsiń, two days.
Bar cando, two months.
Mit' dhao, once.
Pahilte, at first, before.
Ekkalte, at once.

Hol kalom, two years ago.
Pher kalom (*mah kalom*), three years ago.
Tarik, date.
Sedae, formerly.
Tikin, noon, at noon.
Tala ńinda, at midnight.
Jao hilok̇ ayup', every evening.
Jao hilok̇ setak̇, every morning.
Pe mãhã, three days..
Pon serma, four years.
Pahil, first, before.
Lahate, first, before.
Dinam (*ge*), daily.
Dinam hilok̇, every day.

Enan (*re*), a while ago. *Enań* (*re*), do.
Setak̇ setak̇, every morning, or towards morning.
Ayup' ayup', every evening, or towards evening.
Serma serma, every year. *Cando cando*, every month.

Ambas, the time of the change of the moon (also *ambabasia*).

Molok̇ cando, new moon.
Molok̇ tikin, the moon at first quarter.
Kunami, full moon,
Kunami kecak̇, third quarter.

47. Words used adverbially denoting *quantity*.

Aḍi (uḍi), very, very much.
Ḍhertet', much, mostly.
Eken, only.
Baṛic', (lit. bad) very; *bebaṛic'*, exceedingly, awfully.
Thoṛa (-thuṛi), a little.
Bejae, very, extraordinarily.
Nase nase, a little..

48. Words used adverbially denoting *quality* and *manner*.

Besides base-words used adverbially these adverbs are mostly formed by adding certain postpositions or postpositional words, especially *leka*, *lekate*, *kate* and *te*.

Hare phare, *hako pako*, quickly; *bai baite*, slowly; *aḍi leka*, in many ways; *bes lekate*, in a good way, thoroughly; *jute jutete*, in a nice way, carefully; *jormotte*, by force; *gitic' gitic'te*, lying down; *hor horte*, along the road; *barea kate*, in twos; *erekate*, falsely; *sulukte*, in peace, peacefully.

The Pronouns.

49. With certain restrictions Santali may be said to have the ordinary six kinds of pronouns, the personal, the demonstrative, the interrogative, the indefinite, the possessive and the relative pronouns.

The restrictions concern the possessive and the relative pronouns, for which the language has no separate or special pronouns, but makes use of the personal, demonstrative and interrogative pronouns.

With few exceptions the pronouns are treated like ordinary base-words, i. e., they may function as nouns, adjectives and verbs.

Certain demonstrative, interrogative and indefinite ɔnouns show separate forms for the animate and e inanimate.

The Personal Pronouns.

0. Santali has the ordinary personal pronouns for the ree persons, in the Singular, the Dual and the Plural, ith separate forms for the 1st pers. Dual and Plural, cording to whether the speaker includes or excludes the e or those addressed. For the 3rd pers. a demonstative pronoun has in certain cases to be used.

ɔ1. The language has separate forms for the ***independent***, the ***suffixed*** and the ***infixed*** personal pronouns.

	The Independent Forms.	The Suffixed Forms.
Sing. 1st pers.	*iń*, I.	*-iń* or (after single vowel) *-ń*, I.
„ 2nd „	*am*, thou.	*-em* (or *-em*), or (after single vowel) *-m*, thou.
„ 3rd „	*ać*, himself, herself. *uni*, he, she. *ona*, it, that (inanimate).	*-e* (or *-e*, or *-i*,) he, she. Only about animates, except in certain cases for the verbal subject when inanimate.
Dual 1st pers.	*alaṅ* (inclusive), thou and I, we two.	*-laṅ*, thou and I.
„ „ „	*aliń* (*aliń*) (exclusive), he (she) and I, we two.	*-liń*, he (she) and I.
„ 2nd „	*aben* (*aben*), you two.	*-ben* (*-ben*), you two.

Dual 3rd pers.	*ạkin* (*akin*), they two themselves.	*-kin*, they two (only about animates).
	unkin, they two (animate).	
	onakin, those two (inanimate).	
Pl. 1st pers.	*abo*, *abon* (inclusive), we, you and I.	*-bo*, *-bon*, we (inclusive).
,, ,, ,,	*alẹ*, *ale* (exclusive) we, I and they.	*-lẹ*, *-le*, we (exclusive).
,, 2nd ,,	*apẹ*, *ape*, you.	*-pẹ*, *-pe*, you.
,, 3rd ,,	*ako*, they themselves (animates).	*-ko*, they (animates).
	onko, they (animates).	
	onako, those (inanimates).	

52. The *infixed* forms, used in verbal constructions, for the direct and indirect object, are the following :—

Singular	1st	pers.	*-iń-*, *-eń-*, or (after single vowel) *-ń-*.
,,	2nd	,,	*-mẹ-*, *-me-*, or (after *ka*, and as indirect object) *-m-*.
,,	3rd	,,	*-ẹ-*, *-e-* (only used about animates).
Dual	1st	,,	*-laṅ-* (inclusive).
,,	,,	,,	*-liṅ-* (exclusive).
,,	2nd	,,	*-bẹn-*, *-ben-*.
,,	3rd	,,	*-kin-* (only animates).
Plural	1st	pers.	*-bo-*, *-bon-* (inclusive).
,,	,,	,,	*-lẹ-*, *-le-* (exclusive).
,,	2nd	,,	*-pẹ-*, *-pe*.
,,	3rd	,,	*-ko-* (only animates).

Observe the differences between the suffixed and the infixed forms in the Singular.

53. Besides the forms mentioned the language has certain forms of the personal pronouns used to denote possession. There are two sets, one with a *ta* prefixed to the suffixed form (the *a* being lost in the 1st pers. sing.). This form is used partly as a suffixed, partly (in verbal constructions) as an infixed pronoun.

The forms are the following:

Sing.	1st per.	*-tiṅ*, my, mine.
„	2nd „	*-tam*, thy, thine.
„	3rd „	*-tae*, his, her.
Dual	1st pers.	*-talaṅ* (inclusive), mine and thine.
„	„ „	*-tạliṅ* (exclusive), mine and his, or her.
„	2nd „	*-taben*, you two's.
„	3rd „	*-tạkin*, they two's.
Plural	1st pers.	*-tabo, -tabon*, our (inclusive), your and mine.
„	„ „	*-tale* (*-talẹ*), our (exclusive), their and mine.
„	2nd „	*-tape* (*tapẹ*), your.
„	3rd „	*-tako*, their.

54. Besides these the language makes use of the following suffixed personal pronouns, doing service for possessive pronouns:

Sing., Dual and Pl.	1st p.	*-iṅ, -ṅ* (or in one single appellative *-ṅ*), my, our.
„ „ „	2nd p.	*-m* (or in certain cases *-me*), thy, your.
„ „ „	3rd p.	*-t* (frequently intensified to *-ttẹt'*), his, her, their.

The same form is used for all numbers.

55. It will be seen, that the independent pers. pronoun of the third pers. has got a special meaning attached to it, viz. the pronoun and self (or selves); this has resulted

in a demonstrative pronoun being used instead. This special meaning is not attached to the suffixed or infixed forms.

Ińgeń calaḱ tabona, I shall go for us; *idimeae,* he will take you along with him; *ẹrẹkeťleakin,* they (two) deceived us; *babon ạkinkakina?* shall we not make a pair of the two? *hataotakom,* receive what they have; *ạpuń lạiaeme,* tell my father; *eṅgamko ńẹlkedea,* they saw your mother; *ạjitteťe ruạena,* their elder sister became ill; *akogeko idiketkotakoa,* they took their ones away themselves.

The Possessive Pronouns.

56. To render our possessive pronouns the language uses the personal pronouns, with or without a prefix (*ta*) or a postposition, also the interrogative and the demonstrative pronouns.

The independent form of the personal pronouns conveys the idea of a possessive pronoun when it stands as an adjective preceding a word functioning as a noun. When standing coordinate with the following word, it is naturally functioning as the personal pronoun.

A personal pronoun preceding an inanimate noun always stands for our possessive pronoun.

Am hopon, your child; *ale koṛa,* our boy; *ako oṛaḱ,* their house; but *ale hoṛ,* we Santals.

57. When functioning as possessive pronouns the personal pronouns are frequently given a determinative suffix *-iċ, -kin,* and *-ko* for animates, and *-aḱ, -aḱkin* and *-aḱko* for inanimates.

Ińiċ koṛa, my boy; *aboiċ gại,* our cow (as distinguished from somebody else's); *amaḱ oṛaḱ,* your house; *apeaḱ roṛ,* your words, talk.

58. To make the personal pronouns function as possessive ones the postposition *re* may be suffixed, with an *n* added for animates (*ren*), and the determinative suffixes (*ak*, or *an*), for inanimates (*reak*, *rean*). See paras 23 and 24.

Amren gidra, your child ; *ape reak katha*, your story ; *abo reak boge juda*, our circumstances (how we are ; lit. our good otherwise).

59. As regards the so-called genitive infix or suffix (the suffixed form with *ta* prefixed) see para 53.

As regards the suffixed pers. pronouns serving as possessives (*-iń*, *-ń*, *-m*. *-me*, and *t*) see para 54.

Some examples are given to show the use.

Apu-ń, *-m*, my (our), thy (your) father ; *apa-t*, his, her, their father ; *eṅga-ń*, *-m*, *-t*, my, our, thy, your, his, her, their mother ; *kaka-ń*, *-m*, *-t*, my (etc.) uncle (father's younger brother) ; *hopon-iń*, *-me*, *-tet'*, my (etc.) son, child ; *hoṅhar -iń*, *-me*, *tet'*, my (etc.) father-in-law *misera-ń*, *-m*, *-t*, my (etc.) sister (note : a woman has no *misera* ; a woman's sister is *aji-ń*, *-m*, *-t*, my (etc.) elder sister, *boko-ń*, *-m*, *-t* (*kuṛi*), my (etc.) younger sister, or *boeha era*, or something similar).

The Demonstrative Pronouns.

60. The language has a very large number of demonstrative pronouns, differing in form for the animate and the inanimate, also distinguishing distances, having different demonstratives for what is close by and further off, for what is general and what is singled out (identity), besides a separate series for what is on the side.

The demonstrative pronouns proper are compounds, consisting of a demonstrative element with an animate or inanimate determinative pronominal affixed.

61. The *ordinary* demonstrative pronouns are the following:

Animate.	*Inanimate.*
Nui (dual *nukin*, pl. *noko*), this one here close by.	*Noa* (dual *noakin*, pl. *noako*), this thing here close by.
Uni (dual *unkin*, pl. *ọnko*), that one there near.	*Ona* (dual *onakin*, pl. *onako*), that thing there near.
Huni (dual *hunkin*, pl. *honko*), that one there further off.	*Hona* (dual *honakin*, pl. *honako*), that thing there further off.
Ni (for *nii*, dual *nikin*, pl. *neko*), this very one, just this one here, close by.	*Niạ* (dual *niạkin*, pl. *niạko*), this very thing, just this here, close by.
Ini (dual *inkin*, pl. *enko*), just that one, that very one there, near.	*Inạ* (dual *inạkin*, pl. *inạko*), that very thing, just that thing there, near.
Hini (dual *hinkin*, pl. *henko*), that very one, just that one at a distance.	*Hinạ* (dual *hinạkin*, pl. *hinạko*), that very thing, just that, at a distance.
Ạni (dual *ạnkin*, pl. *anko*), that one far off (scarcely ever heard, but frequently used by the Mahles).	*Hana* (dual *hanakin*, pl. *hanako*), that thing far off.
Hạni (dual *hạnkin*, pl. *hanko*), that one far off.	*Nẹ* (dual *nẹkin*, pl. *nẹko*), this very (mostly used adverbially, but also as a demonstrative pronoun.)
Hạ̃i, the same as *hạni*, found only in the singular.	*Nọ* (only in the singular), this.
	Na (only in the sing.), this.

62. It will be seen that there are three sets, with different forms for distances and identity; those pointing to what is close by commencing with *n*, those pointing to what is near commencing with a vowel followed by the same *n*, and those pointing to a distance being the same as the last ones with an *h* prefixed.

The affixed animate determinative is in the sing. *i*, in the dual and plural respectively *kin* and *ko*; the corresponding inanimate determinative is *a* (to which *kin* and *ko* may be added for the dual and the plural).

63. The language has some *intensified* demonstratives, all formed from those with initial *n*.

Animates.	*Inanimates.*
Nŭk'ŭi, this one you see here (only singular, from *nui*).	***Nǭk'ǭe*** (dual *nǭk'ǭekin*, pl. *nǭk'ǭeko*), this thing you see here (from a non-existing *nǫe*, cp. *ǫnę* and *nǫ*).
Nik'ĭ, just this one you see here (only singular; from *ni*).	
Nịk'ại, that very person over there (only singular; from a *nại*, not found in the present-day language; cp. the lateral demonstratives).	***Nẹ̄k'ẹ̄*** (dual *nẹ̄k'ẹ̄kin*, pl. *nẹ̄k'ẹ̄ko*), just this thing you see here (from *nę*, cp. *ęnę*)

64. The *laterally* demonstrative pronouns are formed from those having initial *n* by making this *n* aspirated (*nh*). They are:

Animates.	*Inanimates.*
Nhui (dual ***nhukin***, pl. ***nhoko***), this one here, on the side (corresp. to ***nui***).	***Nhoa*** (dual ***nhoakin***, pl. ***nhoako***), this thing here on the side (corresp. to *noa*).
Nhi (dual *nhikin*, pl. *nheko*), just this one, this very one here, on the side (corresp. to *ni*).	*Nhią* (dual *nhiąkin*, pl. *nhiąko*), just this thing, this very thing, here on the side (corresp. to *nią*).
Nhąi (dual *nhąkin*, pl. *nhąko*), that one at a distance, on the side (corresp. to a not found *nąi*; cf. the intensive *nąk'ąi*).	*Nha* (dual *nhakin*, pl *nhako*), that thing there at a distance, on the side (corresp. to a very rarely used *na*). *Nhawa* (i. e. *nha-a*)=*nha*.

65. The intensified forms of these are

Animates.	*Inanimatess*
Nhũk'ũi, this one you see here on the side (only singular, corresp. to *nũk'ũi*).	***Nhǫ̃k'ǫ̃e*** (dual ***nhǫ̃k'ǫ̃ekin***, pl. ***nhǫ̃k'ǫ̃eko***), this thing you see here on the side, (corresp. to ***nǫ̃k'ǫ̃e***).
Nhĩk'ĩ, just this, this very one you see here on the side (only singular, corresp. to *nĩk'ĩ*).	***Nhę̃k'ę̃*** (dual ***nhę̃k'ę̃kin***, pl. ***nhę̃k'ę̃ko***), this very thing, just this thing you see here on the side (corresp. to ***nę̃k'ę̃***).
Nhą̃k'ą̃i, that person over there on the side (only singular, corresp. to ***ną̃k'ą̃i***).	***Nhãk'ãe*** (dual ***nhãk'ãekin***, pl. ***nhãk'ãeko***), that thing over there on the side (no corresponding form, but cp. ***nha***).

66. Besides the demonstratives already mentioned the language has two sets of demonstratives referring to, drawing attention to *what is seen or heard*. They are the following :

Referring to sight.

Ǫnę (dual *ǫnękin*, pl. *ǫnęko*), that you see there (corresp. to *ona*).

Hǫnę (dual *hǫnękin*, pl. *hǫnęko*), that you see over there (corresp. to *hona*).

Ęnę (dual *ęnękin*, pl. *ęnęko*), just that you see there (corresp. to *iną*).

Hęnę (dual *hęnękin*, pl. *hęnęko*), just that you see over there (corresp. to *hiną*).

Anę (dual *anękin*, pl. *anęko*), that you see over there (corresp. to *ąni*).

Hanę (dual *hanękin*, pl. *hanęko*), that you see there far off (corresp. to *hana*).

Hãe (dual *hãekin*, pl. *hãeko*), the same as *hane* (cp. *hąi*).

Referring to sound.

Ǫtę (dual *ǫtękin*, pl. *ǫtęko*), that, or this one heard there.

Hǫtę (dual *hǫtękin*, pl. *hǫtęko*), that, or that one heard over there.

Ętę (dual *ętękin*, pl. *ętęko*), just that, or this one heard there.

Hętę (dual *hętękin*, pl. *hętęko*), just that, or that one heard over there.

Atę (dual *atękin*, pl. *atęko*), that, or that one heard over there.

Hatę (dual *hatękin*, pl. *hatęko*), that, or that one heard there far off.

Of the above mentioned demonstratives *ǫnę* and *ǫtę*, and to some extent also *ęnę* and *ętę*, have a wider application than to what is seen or heard. *Ǫnę* frequently refers to what is evident and to known or demonstrated facts. *Ǫtę* may also refer to taste, feeling and smell. It may also refer to what is told, a rumour, etc., or the meaning of what is heard.

67. The demonstrative pronouns and adverbs may be intensified by putting a demonstrative element before the pronoun or adverb; this element is always the same as the first syllable of the demonstrative commencing with a vowel or an *h*.

Un uni, the one there; *on ona*, that there; *ǫn ǫnẹ*, that seen there; *han hanko*, those over there; *ǫn ǫṇḍẹ*, just there.

The Demonstrative Adverbs.

68. The language has a large number of demonstrative adverbs, derived from the demonstrative pronouns, and corresponding to ordinary adverbially used words, referring to place, direction, quality, manner and quantity.

Demonstrative adverbs referring to *place* (rest in) are:

Nǫṇḍẹ, here, at this place.	*Nẹṇḍẹ*, just here.
Ǫṇḍẹ, there, at that place.	*Ẹṇḍẹ*, just there, just at that place.
Hǫṇḍẹ, there, at a distance.	
Haṇḍẹ, over there, far off.	*Hẹṇḍẹ*, just there, at a distance.

Those having initial *n* may get this aspirated (*nh*) and then have a meaning pointing to what is on the side: *nhǫṇḍẹ*, here on the side; *nhẹṇḍẹ*, just here on the side.

69. Demonstrative adverbs denoting *direction*.

Nǫtẹ, hither, to this place or part.	*Nẹtẹ*, just to this place.
Ǫntẹ, there, to that place.	*Ẹntẹ*, just to that place.
Hǫntẹ, over in that direction.	*Hẹntẹ*, just over in that direction.
Hantẹ, over in that far off direction.	
Nhǫtẹ, hither on the side.	*Nhẹtẹ*, just hither on the side.
Nhatẹ, over in that direction, off on the side.	

70. The adverbs may be enlarged by adding a postposition, *re* to show rest in, *te* to show direction, and

any other postposition that will suit. ***Nọndẹre***, here in this place; ***ẹndẹre***, just there in that place (this last expression is very frequently used to express 'in that case', 'if that is so').

Nọtẹtẹ, in this direction.
Ontẹtẹ, in that direction.
Họntẹtẹ, over in that direction.
Hantẹtẹ, over in that direction far off.
Nhọtẹtẹ, *nhẹtẹtẹ*, in this direction on the side.
Notẹ sẹc', towards here, in this direction.
Nọtẹrẹ, here in this direction.
Nọtẹ sec'rẹ, in these parts, towards here.
Nẹtẹ khọn, from these parts.

Nẹtẹtẹ, just in this direction.
Ẹntẹtẹ, just in that direction.
Hẹntẹtẹ, just over in that direction.
Nhatẹtẹ, over in that direction far off on the side.
Nhatẹ sẹc', towards that direction away on the side.
Hantẹrẹ, over there in that direction.
Nẹtẹ khọn, just from hereabouts, etc., etc.

71. Demonstrative adverbs denoting *quality* and *manner*.

These are formed by suffixing *ka* to one of the demonstrative elements *non*, *on*, *nen*, *en*, *hon*, *hen* and *han* (with their lateral variations). They are:

Nonka, thus, in this way.
Onka, thus, in that way.
Honka, thus, in that way (further off).
Hanka, thus, in that way, like that far off.
Nhonka, thus, like this on the side.
Nhanka, thus, like that far off on the side.

Nenka, just in this way.
Enka, just in that way (often with a disparaging side meaning).
Henka, just in that way (further off).
Nhenka, thus, just like this on the side.

By adding a postposition, especially *te* or *re*, the special meaning of the adverb mentioned is emphasized. *Onkate*, in that way, so, thus; *enkate*, just in that way, in the condition in which it was found; *enkare*, just so, in such case.

72. By adding *leka*, like, in accordance with, to the adverbs mentioned in the preceding para a fresh demonstrative adverb is formed.

Nonka leka, in this way.
Onka leka, in that way.
Honka leka, in that way.
Hanka leka, in that way, like in that manner far off.
Nenka leka, just in this way, like in this manner.
Enka leka. just in that way, like in that manner.
Henka leka, just in that way, like thus further off.
Nhonka leka, *nhenka leka*, *nhanka leka*, same meanings as above, only with the lateral qualification.

This *leka* may be added to any word, the result being an adverb denoting a way, manner or functioning like that or of that to which *leka* is added.

73. Demonstratives used as adverbs denoting *quantity*.

Nun, so, so much, this much.
Un, that much, so many.
Nin, so, this much, just this much.
In, just so much, that very.

With the corresponding laterally demonstrative adverbs: *nhun*, *nhin*, and *nhạn*.

These demonstrative adverbs are also used about time: then, at that time.

E. g., *nun maraṅ*, so big; *nun serma*, so many years; *un din*, so long a time; *nun jeleṅ*, so long; *nin tirit'*, so much (as shown); *nin hoṛgeako*, they are just so many people; *in kaṭic'*, so small; *in dhao*, so many times; *in gan*, about as much; *in angẹ*, *in ena*, *in anaṅ*, then only, not till then.

74. When adverbially used these demonstratives are followed by an adjective; when taking a postposition they function combined with this as an adverb. The demonstratives mentioned in the preceding para all take postpositions; especially *re* and *te* are of constant occurrence.

E. g., *unre*, then, at that time; *inre*, at that very time; *ninte*, by this time (now gone); *inte*, by that time; *inkote*, by about that time (note the plural suffix *ko*, about the indefinite); *intekote*, by about that time; *unkote*, by about that time.

75. The demonstratives mentined para 74 are with *ạk̇* added used as demonstratives and as demonstrative adverbs. The forms are the following:

Nunạk̇, this much. *Ninạk̇*, just this much.
Unạk̇, that much. *Inạk̇*, just that much.
Hạnạk̇, that much (as that at a distance).
Hạnạṅ, do.

With the corresponding laterally demonstrative forms:
nhunạk̇, *nhinạk̇*, *nhạnạk̇*.

The Interrogative Pronouns.

76. There are two classes of interrogative pronouns, one for animates and one for inanimates; inside each class one pronoun simply singles out, while the other refers to quality and reality.

For animates.

Qkǫe (dual *ǫkǫekin*, pl. *ǫkǫeko*), who, which one.
Cele (dual *celekin*, pl. *celeko*), which, what kind.

For inanimates.

Oka (dual *okakin*, pl. *okako*), what, which one.
Cet' (dual *cet'kin*, pl. *cet'ko*), what.

Okọe and *oka* frequently have *ṭaḱ* (also *ṭa* and *ṭaṅ*) added; *ṭaḱ* signifies the unit, makes the question more pointed.

E. g., *ọkọe kanae?* who is it? *cele hoṛ kanae?* what kind of a person is he? *oka hoṛte?* by which way? *cet'em emaea?* what will you give him? *ọkọe baḍae?* who knows? *celeama ńutum?* what is your name?

77. *Cet' - cet'* preceded by a *ge*, put after words, correspond to 'whether - or', 'both - and'. *Ṭakage cet' poesage cet'*, whether rupees or pice (all of it).

78. *Cele* is often used to introduce a question, translatable with a 'well' or 'how is it'? It is also used adverbially inside sentences to express 'presumably' or 'likely'. *Cele, jarwayenabon sẹbon baṅa,* well, how is it, are we here all or not? *pon hoṛ celeko tahẽkana*, they were, I presume, four persons.

79. *Okor* is an interrogative pronoun, to some extent corresponding to the demonstrative *ọnẹ*; it is used remonstratingly, when a person does not see or find what he is expected to see or find.

Okor, baṅ ńẹlet'a, why, I do not see it; *okoriċ apat hoṛ dọ,* why, where is the father? *okoran tako katha dọ?* where is what they have to say, I do not hear anything.

Interrogative Adverbs.

80. In analogy with the adverbially used demonstratives and demonstrative adverbs the language has also a number of interrogative adverbs of a similar nature, not necessarrily, but mostly a compound of

an interrogative pronoun and a postposition or a post-positionally used word.

81. Referring to *place*:

Oka, where ? (alone, or mostly with a postposition).

Okam dukạna ? where did you go ? *okate ?* whereto ? *okare ?* where ? *oka ṭhen ?* at which place ? *oka khon ?* wherefrom ?

82. Referring to *time*:

Tis (*tisok'*), when ? (referring to time in general, but not the same day); *tin, tinre,* when ? (referring to the time of the day).

Tisem hijuk'a ? when (what day) will you come ? *tinreye calaoena ?* when (at what o'clock) did he go ? *tis khon,* from what time ? *tin jokhẹc' ?* at what time (of the day) ?

83. Referring to *quantity*:

Tin, how much, how many, how big.

Tinạk', how much, how many.

Tin is in this sense always prefixed to a word; standing alone it refers to time.

Tin marań, how big; *tin sạṅgiń*, how far away; *tin tirit'*, how much; *tinạk'e emat'mea*, how much did he give you ?

84. Referring to *manner*:

These are all an interrogative pronoun with *leka*, *lekare* or *lekate* added. *Cet' leka*, in what way, manner; *cet' lekate*, in what way; *cet' lekare*, in what manner, circumstances; *oka leka*, in what manner; *tinạk' leka*, like how many, in how many ways.

The Relative Pronouns (and Relative Sentences).

85. As already remarked the language has no relative pronouns proper and has to make use of other pronouns in stead, or to manage insome other way.

(*a*) The easiest and to a Santal probably the most natural way to render our relative sentences is to take the whole sentence as an attribute to the governing word, omitting all pronouns.

We may have a full sentence, only omitting the finite *a*, or we may have a participial construction, without the verbal subject.

Sen̥en hor̥, the person who went; *ghar̥di jãwãeko aguade kur̥i*, the girl for whom they brought a house-husband.

(*b*) To the above first mentioned construction an *one̥* may be prefixed, *one̥* referring to the whole expression. *One̥m he̥člen hilok'*, the day you came.

(*c*) The interrogative pronouns *okoe* and *oka* (for animates and inanimates respectively), with or without an *one̥* prefixed are used corresponding to 'who', 'which' and 'that'. Such relative sentences may stand before or after the word to which they belong.

Mit' ṭen hor̥, okoe noae kami dar̥eak', a man who can do this; or, just as well, *noae kami dar̥eak' mit' ṭen hor̥*.

(*d*) *Cet'* and *cele* may also be used as relative pronouns, always preceding the governing word. *Cet'e khoj kan ona emaeme*, give him what he wants; *cele coko metae hor̥*, a what do they call him man.

(*e*) The demonstrative pronouns (generally those with initial vowel) and the personal pronouns, always with *one̥* prefixed, may serve as relative pronouns. *Uni kor̥a, one̥ uni ca bagwanteye se̥nlen*, the young man who went to the teagarden; *abon, one̥ abon non̥d̥e̥ menak'bon*, we who are here.

(*f*) The indefinite pronouns *jãhãe* or *jãhãe ǫkǫe* and *jãhã* or *jãhã oka* (for animates and inanimates respectively) may also serve as relative pronouns, preceding the governing word.

86. A relative sentence proper does not take the finite *a*. It is, however, very frequently heard, especially when the relative sentence comes after the governing word, but also when it comes before this. In this case we have not a relative sentence, but a disjointed full sentence.

The Indefinite Pronouns.

86. There are two indefinite pronouns proper, one for the animate, and one for the inanimate. These may be augmented by adding the interrogative pronouns *ǫkǫe* and *oka* respectively, and also other words.

For animates.	*For inanimates.*
Jãhãe, any one, some one, whosoever.	*Jãhã*, anything, whatever.
Jãhãe ǫkǫe, any one, whosoever.	*Jãhã oka*, anything which, whatsoever.
Jãhãe kahae, any one, some one or other.	*Jãhã kaha*, some or other.
Jãhãe tãhãe, any one, some one or other.	
Jãhãe man tãhãe, some one or other.	

87. The interrogative pronouns when repeated, when getting *cǫṅ* added, or when getting *hǫ̃* or *ge* with a negation attached, function as indefinite pronouns.

E. g., *jãhãeṭak̇*, any one; *jãhãṭak̇*, whatever, anything; *jãhãn janwar*, *jãhãn kaṭ*, any kind of animal, any kind of timber;

jãhãnić (*jãhãnkin*, *jãhãnko*), any one; *jãhãnãk̇* (*-kin*, *-ko*), anything;

jãhã tinạk̇, howsoever much (or many); *dal jãhãnkemako*, they may beat you or do something to you; *ńẹl jãhãn akat'am*, have you chanced to see it (at any time?

Ǫkǫe cǫṅ, somebody, unknown who, whoever it may be.

Cele cǫṅ, do., unknown which.

Cet' cǫṅ, something or other, unknown what.

Oka cǫṅ, something or other, unknown which.

Ǫkǫe hõ baṅ, no one (lit. who also not).

Cele hõ baṅ, no one, not a soul.

Oka hõ baṅ, nothing at all.

Cet' hõ baṅ, nothing.

Ǫkǫege bako hẹćlena, not a single one came; *cet'ge alom rọṛa*, do not say a word; *ǫkǫe ǫkǫe dǫko mẹna*, some people say; *oka oka jaegare*, in sundry places, here and there; *ǫkǫeko dǫko baḍaea*, *ǫkǫeko dǫ baṅ*, some know, others don't.

88 Indefinite *Pronominals*:

Adǫm, some (animate and inanimate, taking plural animate determinative suffix, and inanimate do. in singular and plural); *adǫm adǫm*, some; *adǫmko*, *adǫm adǫmko*, *adǫmak̇*, *adǫmak̇ko*, *adǫm adǫmak̇ko*; *adǫm hǫṛ*, some people; *adǫm dare*, some trees; *adǫm dǫ - - adǫm dǫ*, some - - others.

Adha, half; *adhan*, lit. the half, some, some - -others; *adhan menak̇koa*, *adhanko calaoena*, some are here, some have gone.

Baje, some, some - - others (not used by all in this meaning).

Eṭak̇ (*-ić*, *-kin*, *-ko*, with parallel form *eṭagić*), another, others; *eṭak̇ak̇* (*eṭagak̇*) (*-kin*, *-ko*), another, others (inanimate). *Eṭak* is used about both animates and inanimates.

Kichu, some, a little; *kichu kichui phạrịạ ńõk akana*, he has improved a little; *je kichu*, whatever (little).

Ar (commonly used as a conjunction to signify 'and') is also used as a pronominal signifying 'more', 'others'; also doubled, *ar arko*, others. Used about both the animate and the inanimate. *E. g.*, *ar ẹmokme*, give more; *ar hoṛko*, other people (additional to already mentioned ones). Especially common combined with *hõ* (*arhõ*), also, again, more.

Ạḍi (with parallel forms *uḍi* and *ạṛi* or *uṛi*), mostly used as an adverb, but also as a pronominal meaning much or many.

89. The following three words should be remembered, functioning as pronominals: *iạ*, *eman* and *tan*.

Iạ functions as a kind of reference pronominal when the speaker from some cause or other does not remember the proper word, that should have been used, or when the speaker from delicacy or the like does not wish to use a word. *Iạ* is always constructed as the word referred to would be.

Eman functions as a kind of indefinite pronominal referring to somebody or something similar to what is mentioned or tacitly implied. It may function as a noun (always in the plural), but mostly as the second part of a compound, in this case corresponding to 'such like', 'that kind'. Especially with *ten* and *teak* added *eman* (*emanten*, *emanteak*) functions as a noun or adjective translatable with 'such like', 'and so on', 'etc.'

Tan has always a determinative suffix added (*tạnic'*, *tankin*, *tanko* for animates, and *tanak'*, *tanakko* for inanimates). It may be translated 'such like', 'that kind', 'something like'.

Indefinite Pronominal Adverbs.

90. Some of the indefinite pronouns, without or with postpositions, singly or as special compounds, may be adverbially used. It is especially the *jãhã* (with compounds) that is so used. The following are examples only, not a complete list.

Jãhã gem calak', wherever you go; *jãhãre*, wherever; *jãhãte*, wheresoever: *jãhã sẹc'*, in whatsoever direction; *jãhã khon*, from wheresoever; *jãhã tinạk'*, whatsoever, however much; *jãhãtinre*, at any time during the day; *jãhãtisre*, at any time, whensoever; *jãhãtis jãhãtis*, now and then; *jãhãtin jãhãtinre*, now and then in the course of the day; *jãhã leka (te)*, in some way or other; *jãhã kãhã*, here and there.

The Verb.

General remarks.

91. Every Santal word may function as a verb.

When functioning as a verb, the base word itself is not altered.

The exceptions from this rule are only apparent, the alterations being due to the want of applying a special meaning to a word; it really has nothing to do with verbal conjugation.

When a word functions as a verb certain accessories are needed, added to the baseword, as required, viz. a subject, a tense or other suffix, and, in the ordinary finite verb the finite *a*; to these an object infix (for the direct or the indirect object) and a possessive infix may be added.

92. As regards the subject: When animate this has always to be shown in the form of a suffixed personal pronoun; this is added to the word immediately preceding the verb, if there is any such in the sentence, or it may be attached to the end of the the verb. Even when the subject is a personal pronoun it has as subject to be repeated in its suffixed form.

When inanimate the subject is not shown. When, however, an actor or a force is supposed to be behind and to be the real cause of the action, the 3rd pers. sing. of the suffixed pers. pronoun may be and generally is used to indicate this agent. This is especially to be remarked, when natural phenomena are described. This subject pronoun only occurs in the Active, and in the Medium when this has active meaning.

E. g., horoko casa, they cultivate rice; *calak'am? hẽ, iṅiń calak'a*, will you go? yes, I shall go (*calak'ań* may be said, bnt not *iń calak'a*; it would have to be *iṅiń calak'a*, or *hẽń calak'a*); *holae dak'ket'a*, it rained yesterday; *hola dak' ńũrena*, rain fell yesterday; *amak' ghaṭkogeye baṛic'ket'mea*, your misdeeds ruined you.

93. As regards the verbal suffixes: To show tense or mood, different for the different voices, suffixes are added to the base-word. The language has three sets, one set for the direct object, one for the indirect object and one for intentional action. These will be shown in detail further on.

94. The finite verb gets an *a* added.

95. In the Active an animate object is always shown in the verb by an infixed personal pronoun, whether the object is direct or indirect (there is no difference in the form of the pronoun); an inanimate object is not shown, except in certain tenses (which will be shown below) with indirect object and in the Intentional.

96. Besides the infixes mentioned that are obligatory, a possessive infix may be added, in the Active after the object infix, in the Medium and the Passive after verbal the suffix.

A Santal verb consequently consists of

base-word + verbal suffix + object infix (in the Active and if animate) + possessive infix (optional) + the finite a *+ subject pronoun.*

97. The base-word is not altered; but in certain cases fresh base-words are formed from the old one, when a special meaning is required. The base-word itself may in this way be altered to express Peformative and Reciprocal action.

The Performative Base.

98. When it is wanted to show that the base-word is to convey the idea of active performance, the base may be altered in one of two ways:

(a) By reduplication of the first consonant and its following vowel; this is restricted to words having initial consonant. *E. g.*, *bebenao*, from *benao*, to make; *dadal*, from *dal*, to strike; *sisi*, from *si*, to plough; *lạlại*, from *lại*, to tell.

(b) By infixing an *k̓* after the first vowel of a word. This may be done with all base-word, and must be done with words having initial vowel. *E. g.*, *bek̓nao*, from *benao*, to make; *ạk̓gu* from *ạgu*, to bring; *ạk̓-ạulạu*, from *ạulạu*, to bring into disorder.

A combination of the two methods is sometimes heard.

99. Note: words with aspirated initial consonant keep this as initial in the fresh word, but does away with the aspiration in the second syllable. *Jhajaṛ*, from *jhaṛ*, to exorcise.

Words with initial dipthong infix the *k̓* after the first vowel, the whole diphthong following the *k̓*. *Ak̓aosan*, from *aosan*, to relieve.

In compound words the *k̓* may be inserted or the reduplication effected in the principal part of the compound, or when such is not obvious, where convenient. *Nijọjọr*, from *nijọr*, weak; *kurumuk̓ṭu*, from *kurumuṭu*, exert oneself; *puruchucun*, besides *puk̓ruchun*, from *puruchun*, to propitiate.

100. The Performative does not take verbal suffixes; it is found in the Indeterminate or Future and in the Definite Present and do. Imperfect (i. e. the base alone or with *kan* or *kan tahẹkan* added). A pronominal genitive infix may follow.

101. With the determinative suffix (*-id*, *-ak̓*) added the Performative is used to show the agent, the doer, the person whose profession is denoted by the word,

and, in the case of inanimates, that which performs, or the implement with which an action is performed. *-teaḱ* added to the Performative base is a common way of naming an implement.

Raranič, one who applies medicines, a doctor; *bebenaoko*, the makers, builders; *Bebenaoič*, the Creator; *ạḱsulič*, the supporter; *kuḱṭamaḱ*, anything to hammer with; *ma·naḱteaḱ*, anything with which to cut, an axe; *haḱlateaḱ*, that by which refund is made.

102. The Performative is Active; when a form is required to show a corresponding pure Passive this may be done by reduplicating the Medium and Passive suffix of the Indeterminate, viz. *oḱ*; *oḱoḱ* becomes *ogoḱ* (or after words with final vowel *goḱ*).

Ńẹloḱa, it will be seen; *ńẹlogoḱa*, it is visible; *sioḱaḱ*, what ploughs, the plough; *siogoḱaḱ*, what is ploughed, the field.

The Reciprocal Base.

103. A Reciprocal base is formed by infixing a *p* after the first vowel of a word; as a rule this vowel is fully repeated after the *p*.

In reciprocal bases formed from disyllabic bases the vowel may sometimes be omitted after the *p*.

In a few words with *e* or *i* in the first and *ọ*, *o* or *u* in the second syllable the vowel of the second syllable is spoken after the *p*.

Words with a diphthong in their first syllable infix the *p* after the first vowel and repeat the diphthong after the *p*.

When the first vowel of a disyllabic word is resultant, both the vowel preceding and following the *p* becomes the corresponding ordinary vowel (*ạ* becomes *a*), except in monosyllabic words, words with initial diphthong and in disyllabic words with final *ại*.

Ńẹpẹl, see each other; from *ńẹl*, see, *oporom* and *oprom*, recognize each other, from *orom*, recognize; *ńẹpẹl oprom hoṛ*, an acquaintance; *dapram*, meet, from *daram*; *bapla*, marriage, from *bala*.

Ẹpẹhẹp', mutually begin, from *ẹhẹp'*, begin; *iputut'*, from *itut'*, apply sindur to the forehead of a girl; but *sipiboṛ*, from *siboṛ*, strip and rob.

Upuihar, mutually long for, from *uihar*; *ạpạulạu*, from *ạulạu*, bring into disorder; *lạpại*, tell one another, from *lại*, tell; *lạpạṛhại*, fight one another, from *lạṛhại*.

Apasul, mutually support, from *ạsul*; *tapaṅgi*, wait for one another, from *tạṅgi*.

104. This form denotes reciprocality, to do the same to one another, to meet in performing similar action.

105. The form is often used to show a collection of people having the same occupation or station, a class of such people.

Hapṛamko, the ancestors; *rapajko*, the class of kings; *mapañjiko*, the village headmen as a class; *kạpṭičko*, the small ones; *gipitič*, the camping place of the annual hunt.

The Repetitive Base.

106. Verbal bases may be formed by repetition of the single word. Any word functionig as a base, also the Performative and the Reciprocal may be repeated. The verbal suffixes are added to the second word.

The meaning of this form is primarily repetition or continued performance. It may also convey the idea of distribution.

Repetition may be an attempt at doing a thing. This form may consequently convey a conative meaning; this, is especially the case, when the Repetitive base has the suffixes of the Intentional in the Active. With the suffix of the Simple Past Active of the Intentional we have a form that denotes an unsuccessful attempt.

Taṛam taṛampe, walk steadily on, hurry up; *ẹm ẹmokme*, give out, continue to give; *baṅ dare dare akana*, it has not as yet grown much; *tahẹn tahẹnte*, by remaining, as time passes; *bicạr bicạrteko aṅgaket'a*, they passed the night until dawn in judging; *ńam ńamkat'koae*, he tried in vain to find them; *hẹc' hẹc'-kat'aṅ, baṅ hec' daṛeat'a*, I tried to come, but could not manage.

---

107. Verbal bases are constantly formed by adding a second word to a base word, the two words forming a verbal base. The second word may be any suitable word. We shall here mention two of these compound bases, that are of so common and constant occurrence as to require being specially dealt with, viz. the Causative or Permissive base and the Inchoative.

The Causative and the Permissive.

108. By adding *oco* to the conjugational base a Causative or a Permissive is formed.

Constructed with direct object the form is Causative, with indirect object it is Permissive. The Permissive implies permission, leave to do, or absence of any attempt to prevent an act taking place.

Kiriń ocokedeań, I made him buy it (e. g. the bullock); *kiriń ocoadeań*, I let him buy; *ńe̥l ocokom*, make them see it, show it to them; *ńe̥l ocoakom*, let them see it; *ńe̥l ocoyenae*, he was caused to be seen; *ran ocok'me*, be medically treated (by somebody).

109. *Oco* is frequently used to show the sufferer, the subject of the Passive; the Performative is in a corresponding case used to show the actor. *Dadalić do̥ nui, dal ocoyic' do̥ uni*, the one who gave the beating is this one, the one who was beaten is that one.

The Inchoative.

110. By adding the postposition *lạgit'* (or *lagat'*) to the Indeterminate tense of any verb a construction called the Inchoative is formed.

The principal word functions as a verb, taking direct or indirect object infix with or without an added genitive infix, or the Medium or Passive suffix of the Indeterminate. To this constructed base *lạgit'* is added.

The Inchoative takes the suffixes of the Medium, the tenses occurring being the Indeterminate and from this formed tenses by adding *kan* and *kan tahe̥kan*.

The meaning conveyed by this form is that the verbal subject is on the point of doing what the principal word denotes.

Sabe lagidok kan tahẽkanae, he was just on the point of catching him; *seta doe geger lagadok kana,* the dog is going to bite; *senok lagidok kanae,* he is on the point of starting; *agui lagidok kanae,* he is just going to bring it.

The Verb Substantive.

111. The verb Substantive or the Copula is in Santali *kan.* A paradigm of this is given here below; it will show, how the finite *a* occurs and how the subject pronoun is affixed to this, in case it is not affixed to a word immediately preceding the verb.

Singular	*kan-a-ń,*	I am.
	kan-a-m,	thou art.
	kan-a-e,	he, she is (animate).
	kan-a,	it is, they are (inanimate, identical for all numbers).
Dual	*kan-a-laṅ,*	we two are (i. e., thou and I, inclusive).
	kaa-a-liń,	we two are (i. e., he (she) and I, exclusive).
	kan-a-ben,	you two are.
	kan-a-kin,	they two are.
Plural	*kan-a-bo (bon),*	we are (i. e., you and I, inclusive).
	kan-a-le,	we are (i. e. they and I, exclusive;
	kan-a-pe,	you are.
	kan-a-ko,	they are.

112. *Kan* has not the meaning of existing; nor does it signify remaining or staying. For these concepts Santali has other words.

It cannot stand alone, but must always be attached to another word denoting the concept to which it refers. It can never precede the word or words to which it refers, but must always and immediately follow this or these.

113. To some extent corresponding to *kan* which refers to actual or supposed present time the language has *tahẽkan* referring to the past. *Tahẽkan* denotes an incomplete, an unfinished or a continuous action or state in the past. It generally corresponds to our 'was', 'were'.

Kan and *tahẽkan* ar both used as auxiliaries in verbal construction; *kan* is a pure auxiliary; *tahẽkan* may be an independent verb.

The Verbal Voices.

114. Verbal conjugation is effected by suffixes added to the base, different for the different tenses and voices. The Santal verb has three Voices, the Active, the Medium and the Passive. The Medium and the Passive suffixes are identical.

The Medium and the Passive suffixes may have a reflexive meaning, and the Medium suffixes may be used in analogy with the Deponent verbs of the classical languages.

The Verbal Suffixes.

115. The Santal language has three sets of suffixes, viz.,

(*a*) for action pure and simple, transitive with a direct object, or intransitive. All voices.

(*b*) for action with an indirect object. Active, and Medium with a reflexive meaning.

(*c*) for showing action with a purpose. All voices.

116. Suffixes are found

(1) for the Indeterminate and the Future (in the Medium or Passive; in the Active no suffix except in certain cases, as detailed below);
(2) for the Present;
(3) for the Past, *a*) performed, *b*) performed, but finished or superseded, *c*) performed and continuing in its results;
(4) for the Preliminary and the Conditional;
(5) for the Optative or Desiderative.

Certain tenses are formed by adding *kan*, *tahẹ̄kan* and *kan tahẹ̄kan*, as will be seen below.

The Verb with direct object.

The Indeterminate and the Future.

117. In the Active there is no suffix; the base is unaltered. To form a finite verb all that is needed is a subject and an object (shown, if animate, by an infixed pers. pronoun; if inanimate, not shown) and the finite *a*.

There are two exceptions: verbs with final single vowel when having an inanimate object get an *e* or an *i* added (*e* when the final vowel is *a*, *o* or *ǫ*, and *i*, when the final vowel is *ạ* or *u*). Verbs with final checked consonant have this changed to its full corresponding voiced consonant (*k̓* to *g*, *č* to *j*, *p̓* to *b* and *t̓* to *d*) when having inanimate object. The same word functioning as an intransitive verb is not altered.

In the Medium and the Passive *ok̓*, or after single final vowel, also after *ao* and *ạu*, only *k̓* is suffixed.

118. The Indeterminate is used to denote the functioning of a word as a verb without reference to any special time.

It is used to denote inherent qualities, general principles, universally accepted statements. Further regularly occurring actions or happenings, general customs or habits and recurring natural phenomena.

It corresponds for the same meanings to the English Present.

119. The same form functions also for the *Future*, for which the language has no separate tense.

E. g., *jelko jọma*, they eat (or will eat) meat; *din hilok'ko jhogṛak̓a*, they are quarrelling every day; *noa churi dọ lasera*, this knife is sharp; *noa họtọt' dọ haṛhat'a*, this pumpkin is bitter; *utui haṛhada*, she will make the curry bitter; *oṛak̓reye tahẹna*, he stays at home (or, will stay); *dadalae*, he is in the habit of beating; *ẹmok̓ae*, he gives (or will give); *ńẹlok̓a*, it will be seen (or is seen); *dak'ko lọlọea*, they will heat the water; but *dak' dọ lọlọa* (*lọlọwa*), the water is hot.

120. A special use of the Indeterminate Medium suffix should be noted. With the determinative suffix added the form is used as a name, where we should use a regular noun. *Rajok̓ko*, the zemindars, those whose position or work entitles them to be called so; *eṅgat apatok̓ko*, parents; *mạńjhik̓ko*, the village headmen (as a class).

The Indefinite Present.

121. This tense occurs only in the Active and is formed by adding *et'* to the base, followed by the object

infix, if any. The *t'* is before an object infix with initial vowel always, and otherwise before the finite *a* often, changed to *d*.

The tense is used to denote a present unfinished act without special reference to the present moment. The tense is often used, when an exact expression would seem to demand the Definite Present.

Daledińae, he beats me; *idiyet'kotaeae*, he is taking his ones away; *hoṛoko rọhọeyet'a*, they are planting rice.

The Definite Present.

122. Formed by adding in the Active *kan* to the Indefinite Present, and in the Medium and the Passive *kan* to the Indeterminate Medium or Passive.

This tense is used to denote what is being done at the present moment (or the time referred to by the speaker); it is also used about what is always, constantly being done.

Gidrạye rak̓et' kana, the child is crying; *Candoe ńẹlet'bon kana*, God is seeing us.

The Indefinite Imperfect.

123. Formed by adding *tahẽkan* to the Indefinite Present. Only in the Active. Used to denote a commenced, but unfinished action in the Past without stress on the moment, something happening in the Past. It is also used to denote what was customary in the Past.

Din kalọm guhumle caset' tahẽkana, last year we were cultivating wheat; *noa bandre hak̓ole sap̓et'ko tahẽkana*, we were catching fish in this tank; *sedae jug-re hor do buluṅko benaoet' tahẽkana*, in olden times Santals were in the habit of making salt.

The Definite Imperfect.

124. Formed by adding *tahẽkan* to the Definite Present.

Meanings: what was stated of the Definite Present transferred to the Past.

Hakoe sap'et'ko kan tahẽkana, he was occupied catching fish; *jelko sendrayede kan tahẽkanre mit'ṭen banako ńamkedea*, as they were chasing a deer they met a bear; *daka isinok' kan tahẽkantakoa*, their rice (food) was being cooked; *noṇḍe khon orak' do ńẽlok' kan tahẽkana*, from here the house was to be seen.

The Simple Past.

125. Formed by adding in the Active *ket'*, and in the Medium and the Passive *en*, to the conjugational base. The *t'* is or may be changed to *d* like the *t'* of the Present suffix.

This tense is used to denote that what the base signifies has been performed, the Simple Past without complications; the act is done.

The Simple Past is not used with a negation, when this functions as such.

Mẽnket'ae, he said; *potame ṭuṭikedea*, he shot the dove (with an arrow); *janumiń rokena*, I was pricked by a thorn; *goe'enae*, he died.

126. The Simple Past with *ge* in stead of the finite *a* is often used in descriptive language; the actual act may belong to any time; the narrator simply sees the act performed. This form has been called Contingent, also a Hypothetical Future.

The Anterior Past.

127. Formed by adding in the Active *let'*, and in the Medium and the Passive *len*, to the conjugational base.

This tense is used to denote that something was done or happened previous to some other event. It may be used to describe historic events of long ago. Or it is used to describe a past action, the effect of which has been nullified, neutralized, superseded or revoked, formally or by a subsequent action or event.

Lạiako, Saharjuṛiko ato maṛaṅlet'a, they tell, that they first founded the Saharjuṛi village ; *idiledeaṅ, arhọe hẹc' ruạṛena,* I took him away, he has again returned ; *ṅẹlledeaṅ,* I saw him (but lost sight of him).

The Anterior Pluperfect.

128. Formed by adding *tahẽkan* to the Anterior Past. The tense is used to denote that something had been done or had happened, but had been neutralized, superseded or revoked in the Past. The tense is also used to denote a conative or frustrated act in the Past.

Cet' lạgit'em sẹn len tahẽkana, for what purpose had you gone ; *Asamtele' sẹnlen tahẽkana,* we had gone to Assam ; *idilede tahẽkanako, adọ nuigeye ạgu ruạṛkedea,* they had taken him away, then this one brought him back.

The Optative.

129. Formed by adding in the Active *ke,* and in the Medium and the Passive *kok',* to the base.

The Optative is used to express a wish or willingness on the part of the subject; it is also used to express a prayer in the form of a question. It is used also to express what the subject may be willing to do, provided certain conditions are fulfilled.

Nui ḍaṅgram ạkriṅkea (note *ke* for *kee*), would you sell this bullock? *mit' ṭakam ẹmkiṅa* (note *kiṅ* for *keiṅ*), would you give me one rupee? *nọṇḍẹm tahẽkok'a*, would you like to stay here? *amem sẹnlenkhan iṅ hõṅ sẹnkok'a,* if you go, I should also like to go.

The Anterior.

130. Formed by adding in the Active *le*, and in the Medium and the Passive *len* to the base.

This tense is used to denote an action or a state that takes place or exists previous to something else. It may be priority in time, a possible previous action or a condition that has to be fulfilled, before something else will or can take place.

Except in connection with the negation *ọhọ* this form is not used with the finite *a*.

Ohọṅ lạilea, I shall certainly not tell; *ọhọe ẹmlema,* he will not give you; *ọhọko cekalena,* nothing will happen to them; *ti aloe sap'letiṅ khan dọṅ ṅurhạkok'a,* if he had not taken hold of my hand, I might have fallen down; *ṭakam ẹmle nạhĩ,* only when you give the money; *rọṛlere dhũndgeye bẹṅgẹda,* when he is upbraided, he sees indistinctly (scolding makes him downcast).

The Imperative.

131. The Imperative is formed by adding the infixed forms of the personal pronoun 2nd pers. sing.,

dual or pl., as may be required, to the Indeterminate in all voices. In case there is an object infix or a genitive infix these are attached to the base and come immediately before the subject pronoun.

The Imperative is as to meaning not different from that of other languages.

Aguime, bring it; *agukoben*, you two bring them; *hijuk'tabonpe*, please come and join us; *noare sabok'me*, take hold of this; *idikom*, take them away.

The Anterior Imperative.

132. An Anterior Imperative is formed by adding the subject pronoun to the suffixes of the Anterior, in the Active to *le*, in the Medium and the Passive to *len*. As to infixes, what was said regarding the simple Imperative holds good.

The Anterior Imperative denotes that what is ordered is to be done before something or anything else is done or happens. It is very commonly used, especially when something is wanted done immediately.

Daka jomlem, adolañ calak'a, take your food first, then we shall go; *hec'lenme*, come at once.

The Prohibitive.

133. The Imperative is not used to express prohibition; the negation *alo* with the finite Future is used instead. The prohibition may be softened down by using *ma* in stead of the finite *a*.

Alom calak'a, don't go; *alo se onka dom rora*, don't, pray, speak in that way; *nonde alo bareko hijuk' ma*, may they not come here.

The Accidental Past.

134. Formed by adding *ken* to the conjugational base, and apparently used only in connection with certain words denoting going and coming, eating, drinking, sitting and standing up. It does not take the finite *a*, but may have *ge* instead.

The suffix has a double meaning; it may convey the idea, that the actor has done something to his personal satisfaction or pleasure; an idea of the unexpected or accidental is often added.

Jǫmken, ńũken, hạ̃i torae calaoena, having had his fill of food and drink, see there he went off; *dãṛã dãṛãte ackageń sẹnken tạrup' dander ṭhen*, wandering about I came unawares to a leopard's den.

Verbal constructions with indirect object.

General remarks.

135. For the verb with indirect object the language has a separate set of tense suffixes in the Active and the Medium. There is no Passive.

There are no suffixes for the Indefinite Present and do. Imperfect; the suffixes of the Optative and the Anterior are identical with the suffixes of the verb with direct object.

136. The tenses correspond as to time to those with direct object, except where noted here below.

The difference between this set of suffixes and those already dealt with is in the meaning, the relation of the verbal action to its object. With direct object, the object of the action is directly affected. With indirect object the action is performed with the intention that it is to have special reference or application to somebody or something mentioned ; the act is done with a result for, to or in connection with somebody or something.

The Medium has a reflexive meanings, the action is done for the subject.

The construction with indirect object presupposes a direct object for the action, the indirect object being the person or thing to which the result of the action (the direct object) is applied.

Direct and indirect object infixes cannot be inserted at the same time ; with direct object the indirect object, if any, may be mentioned in the sentence with a suitable postposition ; with indirect object, the direct object may be mentioned without any postposition or is implied in the verb itself.

A possessive infix may be added,. referring to the direct or to the indirect object.

In the following the different tense suffixes are mentioned, but the meanings are only exceptionally given, these being understood from the meanings of the corresponding forms of the verb with direct object.

The Indeterminate and the Future with indirect object.

137. The verbal suffix is in the Active *a*, to which the infixed pronoun is added, when the indirect object is animate; when it is inanimate it is expressed by

an -*k'* added to the *a*; instead of this *k* a possessive pronominal infix may also be used.

In the Medium the suffix is *joṅ* (always pronounced *jọṅ*).

Kuṛạiko emakoa, they (will) give them their wages; *lạiaeako*, they will tell him; *ḍaṅgrako siakoa*, they use bullocks for ploughing; *bẹṅgẹt'ak'takoae*, he will have a look at what they have; *ẹmọk'ge baṅatakoa*, they will refuse to give; *cet'joṅae*, he will learn; *nẹs dọe ńamjoṅa*, he will find for himself this year (viz., a wife; he will marry).

The Present and the Imperfect with indirect object.

138. With indirect object there is only one Present and one Imperfect, viz. the Definite Present formed by adding the Verb Substantive *kan* to the Indeterminate, and the Definite Imperfect by adding *tahẹkan* to the Present. The forms combine the meanings of both the Indefinite and the Definite Present or Imperfect.

Dak' jọrọak' kana, water (rain) is falling down on it; *noa kũi reak' dak'le ńũak' kana*, we are drinking water from this well; *paṅcateye emako kana*, he is giving it to them as a temporary loan; *cedak'pe bọlọatae kana?* why do you enter his (quarters)? *bachaojoṅ kanako*, they are choosing for themselves; *jọme idiako kan tahẹkana*, she was taking food out to them; *dareṅ bẹṅgẹt'ak' kan tahẹkana*, I was looking at the tree; *jọmjoṅ kan tahẹkanako*, they were eating.

The Simple Past with indirect object.

139. This tense is formed by adding in the Active *at'* (followed by an infixed pronoun, if the indir. object is animate, otherwise nothing), and in the Medium *an* to the conjugational base.

Dak'e dulat'a, he poured water on it; *laiadiñae*, he told me; *pea gotec'e gidrawana*, he got three children.

The Anterior Pluperfect with indirect object.

140. This tense is formed by adding *tahēkan* to the Simple Past with indir. object.

Laiat'ko tahēkanañ, I had told them; *kiriñan tahēkanae*, he had bought.

The Optative with indirect object.

141 The suffixes are the same as for Optative with direct object, in the Active *ke* and in the Medium *kok'*.

Mit'tec' kicric'em emkiña, would you be willing to give me a piece of cloth? *rinte takam emkelea*, would you give us money as a loan?

The Anterior with indirect object.

142. In the Active the suffix is *le*, the same as for the Anterior with direct object; in the Medium the suffix for the Simple Past with indirect object may be used to express the Anterior, not, however, with the finite *a*.

Bin damte ohoñ emlekoa, I shall certainly not give it to them without being paid for it; *hape joangeñ, adobon calak'a*, wait, I shall first have my food, then we shall go.

The Imperative with indirect object.

143. The Imperative is formed by adding the infixed form of the pers. pronoun of the 2nd pers. sing., dual or plural to the constructed Indeterminate with indirect object, in the Active and the Medium, the pers. pr. taking the place of the finite *a* and the subject pronoun of the finite tense.

Jǫm emakom, give them food; *sǫn ocoaeme*, let him go; *juțuc'ak'taeme*, add to what he has; *bęngęț'atakinpe*, look at what they two have; *ńęljońme*, look out for yourself.

The Anterior Imperative with indirect object.

144. Formed, like the Imperative, from the Anterior with indirect object.

Nią ńęllem, have first a look at this; *daka jowanpe*, have first your food.

The Prohibitive with indirect object.

145. The constructed Future with *alo* as negation. In stead of the finite *a ma* may be used, signifiying moıe a wish than an interdict.

Alom lǫiaea, don't tell him; *alope kuŗhiąjońa*, don't be lazy; *alo baŗęko calaǩ ma*, may they not go.

The Intransitive Verb.

146. When a verb is intransitive there is naturally no object infix. In connection with the intransitive verb the following should be noted:

Conjugational bases with final checked consonant keep this and never alter it to its corresponding voiced full consonant.

Beret'ae, he will stand up; *beredae*, he will put something on end; *beret'me*, stand up.

Conjugational bases with final single vowel do not, when intransitive, have an *e* or an *i* suffixed to the Indeterminate, as is the case with such a verbal base when it has an inanimate direct object.

The euphonic vowel between the final single vowel and the finite *a* is *w* (except in words ending in *i* or *e*, where a slight *y*-sound may be heard).

Dak'ko lǫlǫea, they will warm the water; but *dak' lǫlǫwa*, the water is warm.

The Intentional Form of the Verb.

General remarks.

147. Besides the two sets of verbal suffixes already mentioned the language has a third set, conveying the idea of intentional performance.

The base is not altered and keeps its meaning; the relation of the act as to time is not altered. What distinguishes this set of suffixes from the others is that the object of the performance gets special attention; the act is performed with some special intention as to its result.

The ulterior purpose may be one of two. The result of the act is to be final, continuing. This meaning may be observed in all voices, and especially in the Medium and the Passive. Or it may convey the idea that the act is done, the result being intended to remain for a time for some further action. In both cases the meaning conveyed is that the act is done with a special object in view, for a special purpose.

The Intentional suffixes are used when the subject (actor) is an animate, human being. This does not refer to the Passive where the continuance is the preponderant meaning.

The Intentional Active suffixes are used with the Repetitive conjugational base conveying a conative meaning, an attempted, but resultless or frustrated action.

148. The suffixes of the Intentional have, with one exception, as their fundament *ka*, to which *t'* or *n* or *ok'* (*ka+ok'* becomes *kok'*) is added, and to which an *a* may be prefixed.

The Intentional Indeterminate and Future.

149. Formed by adding in the Active *ka*, and in the Medium and the Passive *kok'* to the base.

With inanimate object an *k'* (*kak'*) is added to represent this; this may, however, be omitted when a possessive infix follows.

With animate object the pron. infix is added to *ka*. It should be noted that in the 3. p. sing. the suffix with the animate infix is *kae*, not *kaye*.

Giḍikak'ae, he will throw it away; *baekak'ae*, he will put it by; *peṛañ ạgukakoa*, I shall bring the friends (for some purpose); *koṛabon kolkaea*, we shall send the young man; *ọnḍẹye duṛup'kok'a*, he will sit there (waiting); *rọṛ rọṛkak̃ae, bae pusṭạu daṛeak'a*, he will make vain attempts at speaking, he is unable to speak distinctly; *ikạ kataeae*, he will forgive him.

The Intentional Definite Present.

150. Formed by adding *kan* to the Indeterminate tense. There is no Indefinite tense of the Intentional.

Gạiko idikako kantakoa, they are taking their cows away; *añjọmkak' kanañ*, I am listening (for some purpose); *ikạkatako kanae*, he is always forgiving them; *hapekok' kanae*, he is keeping quiet.

The Intentional Definite Imperfect.

151. Formed by adding *tahẽkan* to the Definite Present.

The Intentional Simple Past.

152. Formed by adding in the Active *kat'*, and in the Medium and the Passive *kan* to the conjugational base.

Apart from *kan* in *tahẽkan* this *kan* does not seem to be used with the finite *a*.

Em ruaṛkat'taeań, I have given what is his back to him; *bochoṛ diniń gupikat'kotama*, I have herded your cattle for a full year; *ranko beste lagao idiaepe, paseće boge kange*, be diligent applying medicine to him, perhaps he may get well again.

The Intentional Anterior Past.

153. Formed by adding *lak'* to the base. Only in the Active and with inanimate object. There is no corresponding Medium or Passive.

Roṛlak'ae, he said it; *oṛak'e raput'lak'a*, he pulled down the house.

The Intentional Anterior Pluperfect.

154. Formed by adding *tahẽkan* to the Intentional Simple Past. Found only in the Active.

Gidra iskulteń idikade tahẽkana, bae tahẽlena, I had taken my child to school (to be taught), he did not stay; *daṛ daṛkat' tahẽkanae, adoe ruaṛena*, he had made an attempt at running away, but came back.

The Intentional Imperative.

155. Formed by adding the infixed form of the pers. pronoun to the Indeterminate. All voices. The inanimate *k'* may be omitted.

Giḍikak'me, throw it away (also *giḍikam*); *idi kakintaben,* take your two ones away; *idi oṭokaeme,* take him away (to some place agreed on) and leave him there; *thirkok'pe,* keep quiet.

The Perfect with direct object.

156. Formed by adding in the Active *akat',* and in the Medium and Passive *akan* to the conjugational base.

None of the other sets of verbal suffixes has any suffix for the Perfect tense. In connection with the Intentional we have an expanded suffix that does service for a Perfect tense. The expanded form is *aka,* to which *t'* or *n* is added.

The Santali Perfect tense denotes a completed action, remaining in its result at the present time or at the the time referred to by the speaker. The perfect presupposes intention, but the predominant meaning conveyed is an act performed and continuing in its result.

The Santali Perfect does not correspond to the socalled Historic Perfect.

Okarem dọhọ akat'a, where have you put it? *jọtọ kuṛiko jāwāe akat'koa,* they have married away all their daughters; *hẹc'akanako,* they are come; *bako tahẽ tayọm akana,* they have not stayed behind.

357. The Perfect tense is often used where we have the Present; this is due, not to any peculiarity of the Santal Perfect, but to the peculiar meaning of the Santal base-word.

Badae akat'koań, I know them (lit. I have learnt to know them); *jąpit' akat'ae*, he is sleeping (lit. he has shut his eyes); *teńgo akanae*, he is standing (lit. he has risen and is continuing in that position); *pątiau akanae*, he believes (lit. he has put belief in).

The Perfect with indirect object.

158. Formed by adding in the Active *akawat'* and in the Medium *akawan* to the conjugational base. The meanings are the same as for the Perfect, only that the object is indirect. No Passive; the Medium is reflexive.

Ląi akawadeań, I have told him; *ranko ęm akawadea*, they have given him medicine; *ągu akawanae*, he has brought for himself.

The Pluperfect with direct and indirect object.

159. Formed by adding *tahẽkan* to the Perfect forms.

The Active Voice with direct object.
Suffix : *akat' - tahẽkan.*

The Active Voice with indirect object.
Suffix : *akawat' - tahẽkan.*

The Medium and the Passive with direct object.
Suffix : *akan tahẽkan.*

The Medium with indirect object.
Suffix : *akawan tahẽkan.*

The tense refers to a state in the Past, the effect of the action remaining at the time referred to, or when something else occurred.

E. g., horoko rohoe akat tahẽkantakoa, they had planted their rice; *lai akawade tahẽkanae*, he had told him;

teṅgo akan tahẽkanae, he was standing (had risen and remained standing); *losot'reye jobe akan tahẽkana*, he was wallowing in the mud; *ṭaka poesa akawan tahẽkanae*, he had acquired some money.

The Continuative Form.

160. A Continuative is formed by the addition to the bare base of *aka*, always followed by *tahen*. The continuative meaning is partly due to *tahen*, to which the tense suffixes are added.

Aka functions like a verb with single final vowel in the Indeterminate, taking object infixes; with one exception, viz., when an object infix for the 3rd p. sing. is to be used, this (- *e*) becomes a diphthong with the *a* (*akae*, and not *akaye*, as in the ordinary verb), in this case following the Intentional.

The *aka* is used with both direct and indirect object and in all voices, as of the Indeterminate.

The tenses used are : the Indeterminate or Future, the Definite Present and the Definite Imperfect. An Imperative is used; an Inchoative may be heard, but is very rare.

The meaning of the Continuative is to continue performing what the base-word denotes, the tense being regulated by the tense of *tahen*.

Sap' akae tahenme, remain keeping hold of him (or it); *beṅget' akawak' tahen kan tahẽkanae*, he was continually looking at it; *horho oco akako tahenme*, make them keep continual watch; *durup' akan tahenae*, he will remain sitting.

Verbal suffixes other than tense suffixes.

161. An *a* is added to the finite verb. This *a* is always the last part of the verb, following the suffix and infixes; the verbal subject, if shown, is added to the *a*, provided it is not affixed to the word immediately preceding the verb (so generally).

With this *a* we have an ordinary statement, something demonstrated; without it there is no demonstration.

When reference is made to only a possibility, when there is doubt, the *a* has to be omitted.

Ọkọe baḍae, who knows (as an indefinite question); but *ọkọeye baḍaea*, who is it who knows; *hijuk'ae*, he will come; but *pasẹt'e hijuk'*, perhaps he will come; *bako ańjọm akat'a*, they have not heard; but *bańḍọko ańjọm akat'*, (I wonder) whether they have heard; *hijuk' cọe bań cọń*, (uncertain) whether he will come or not; *hẹc'len bae*, provided he comes.

162. The finite *a* is not generally used in subordinate clauses, especially never in final clauses, and never when the clause is constructed with a postposition.

An exception is the postpositional *mẹnte*, used in direct or indirect oration; see para 173.

In vivid narratives the *a* is often omitted.

Metakom, ǰẹmọnko calak', tell them to go; *amem calak'khan*, if you go; *ọṇḍẹye tahẽkanre*, while he was there; *lạiat'koae, bae hataoea mẹnte*, he told them he would not take him.

163. In a number of verbal forms some other particle is used in stead of the finite *a*; these particles are *ge*,

ma, *baṅ*, *nā̃hĩ* and *anẹc'* (with its parallel forms *ena* and *enaṅ*), *an*, *anaṅ* and *anẹc'*.

164. *Ge* is an emphatic particle used affixed to any word, that may be emphasized. In certain verbal forms *ge* may take the place of the finite *a*; this is especially the case with the suffixes of the Simple Past, of the Anterior and of the Accidental Past.

With the suffixes of the Simple Past the *ge* emphasizes the performance of an act, but does not refer to any time. This form is not used commencing a narrative, but to show what happens or is done in succession to what has been previously stated. It is also used to state the consequence, what will happen under certain conditions. This form has been called the Contingent, also a Hypothetical Future.

Adọko johar baṛawakoa, adọ mẹrọmko tiạk'kedege, caoleko ghẽṭket'ge, hanko tora ḍerate, so they make their obeisance to them, whereupon they lead the goat away, tie the rice up in their clothes, there they are off to their encampment; *arhõ sẹṅgẹl hạsurena mẹnkhan adọkin sorenge*, when the fire again burns low, they draw near to it.

Added to the suffixes of the Anterior this form is used to express what is purposed to happen before something else is done, or what should or will be done previously to something else.

Aṅjọmletakogeṅ, I must first hear what they have to to say; *hape, jowangeṅ*, wait I must have my food first.

165. *Ma* is a particle conveying an optative, benedictive, precative, cohortative, permissive or admissive sense.

Used with the Imperative *ma* tones the command down to practically a wish.

Iń hǫ̃ń ńẹlko ma, let me also have a look at them; *gọṛọam mako,* may they help you; *alo baṛẹko lạiako ma,* may they not tell them; *hijuk' mako,* let them come; *ona mań rọṛ akat',* why, I have said so; *ona dọ hẹ̃ ma hẹ̃ge,* that is quite so, but -; *iń ma bań sẹnlen,* I did not go (as you know).

166. *Bań* and *nạ̃hĩ* are really identical, the first the Santali negation, the other a negation borrowed from Hindi; but while *bań* (or *ba,* as it commonly is, when a pronoun is affixed to it) is used as the ordinary negation, *nạ̃hĩ* is not ordinarily used, except as shown here below.

Bań and *nạ̃hĩ* are used in stead of the finite *a* added to the suffixes of several tenses (not to those having *kan* or *tahẹ̃kan* added, and not to the Optative). Their use is especially to be noted added to the suffixes of the Anterior in all voices and with direct or indirect object.

When any af these negations is used where the finite *a* should be, the construction denotes that the verb to which it is added is an indispensable condition for the possibility of the implied apodosis.

Dak̃le bań dọle si daṛeak̃a, only when it has rained we shall be able to plough; *ranem ńama, adọm jọmle nạ̃hĩ,* you shall get medicine, but you must take it to get benefit; *dạṛ daṛeak̃ nạ̃hĩ dọe dạṛa,* only in case he is able to run he will do so; *sẹnlen nạ̃hĩ,* only when (if) he goes.

167. *An, anań* and *angẹ̃* are used in stead of the finite *a* in a few verbs (*menak̃* and *bạnuk̃*), especially when constructed inanimate.

Menaka and *menakangẹć*, it is, exists; *bạnuka* and *bạnukanań*, it is not; *bạnugićan*, he is not (here).

168. *Ena*, *enań*, *ẹnẹć*, *anań* and *anẹć* are used in connection with the verb, mostly in the Anterior, without the finite *a*. The particles serve to emphasize the necessary precedence or previousness of the verbal concept; they may be translated 'only when'.

Ran jọmle jirṇule enae guna, only when you have taken and retained medicine it will have effect; *sẹnlen ẹnẹć*, only when (you) go.

Subsidiary clauses.

169. Some relative, consecutive and final clauses are introduced by a conjunction or a word serving for this. Otherwise all subsidiary clauses are formed with the help of a postposition, always coming in the place where the finite *a* should have been.

The most commonly occuring postpositions are: *khan*, *re*, *te*, *iạte*, *ṭhen*, *khon*, *dhạbić'*, *tuluć*, and *sẹlẹt'*.

The postpositions do service for our prepositions and conjunctions.

170. *Khan* corresponds to 'when', and is used about time and condition.

Aṅgayen khanko calaoena, they went when it became dawn; *amem ẹmlekhan iń hǫń ẹmoka*, if you give, I shall also give; *baben jutok kan khan, cet'le mẹna*, as you are not hitting it of together, what can we say.

171. *Re* may be translated 'when', 'during', 'in case' or with a similar word.

Sedaere ṭaka ạuri janamok're, formerly when money had not come into use; *oṛak'reko duṛup' akan tahẽkanre*, when they were sitting in the house; *menaere hõ sẹ bạnugic'te hõ bań cekaka*, it does not matter whether he is here or not; *calak're*, when going.

172. *Te* used in a subsidiary clause denotes the instrumentality or cause, the attending circumstance, the means or manner, and may be translated 'as', 'since', 'when', 'because' or with similar conjunctions.

Amem hẹc'entele rạsk'ayena, we are glad, because you came; *Asamreko sẹṭẹrente ạsulok' reak' bhabna cabayentakoa*, when they arrived in Assam their anxieties in connection with supporting themselves ceased; *hape hapete berel'enteye calaoena*, getting up quietly he went; *calak' calak'teye bindạṛena*, he fell down as he went along.

Te is extensively added to *ka* and *a*, forming the postpositions *kate* and *ate*; see paras 31 and 32.

173. While the postpositions mentioned all presuppose the omission of the finite *a*, there is one, that always demands this, when it follows a verb, viz. *mẹnte*. This means literally 'by saying' and is used in connection with both direct and indirect oration, following the quotation. Following the Imperative there is no *a*.

Now-a-days many under the influence of Bengali or Hindi use *je*, that, introducing the sentence.

E. g., mẹn akawadeań, ọkọe hõ aloe lạiakoa mẹnte, I have told him, that he must not tell anybody; *ọkọe hõ bako rọṛlak'a, ẹm ruạṛk'me mẹnte*, no one said, give it back.

The Infinitive and Participles.

174. The language has no special form or any suffix to show the Infinitive. The Indeterminate of

any conjugational base in any voice and in any set of suffixes may function as an Infinitive; and what we call Infinitive in Santali may take a direct or indirect object infix and also a genitive infix.

E. g., *jǫmko metadea*, they told him to eat; *ǫlǫk̓ paṛhao dǫń bad̥aegea*, I kow to write and read; *eskar tahẹn dǫ bań bogea*, it is not good to live alone; *bạk̓gi dǫ alga dǫ bań kana*, it is not easy to leave off; *gujuk̓e duṛup' akana*, he is sitting to die (is on his deathbed); *dadale chuṭạuk̓a*, he will commence to strike; *hako sap'ko calaoena*, they have gone to catch fish; *hapekok̓e mẹn akawadińa*, he has ordered me to wait; *dil akae tahẹnko uskurket'koa* they urged them to have courage; *calaoenako gitic'*, they went to lie down;

emań dǫ bae rẹbẹnlena, he was unwilling to give me; *onko ạguko manakom*, forbid them to bring those;

lạiapea mẹnteń hẹc'ena, I have come to inform you; *ǫrǫk̓ko kirińko lạgit'*, to buy ploughing cattle.

175. Any word functioning as a verb may also function as a kind of participle. This applies to all voices and tenses.

E. g., *dadal hǫṛ dǫ nui*, *ar dal ocoyenic' dǫ huni*, the beater is this one and the one beaten is that one over there; *mǫn dukok̓ko dǫko calaoena*, these who had grief are gone; *ńamkedeyic'* (or *ńamkede hǫṛ*) *dǫe okayena*, what has become of the one who found him (or may also mean, who was found); *mẹrǫm kirińkeko hǫṛ dǫ bạnuk̓koa*, there is none wanting to buy the goats; *kạk̓mi kan tahẽkanic'*, the one who was working; *ruạ jaṛao akan hǫṛ*, a person down with fever; *dag hilok̓*, a day with rain; *noko kuṛi dǫ d̥ạṅgṳạko sẹ jãwãeko kanako?* are these girls spinsters or married ones (lit. husbanded ones)?

Compound verbal bases.

176. The language makes constant use of compound verbs, two or more words placed side by side. In a few cases such words may stand on an equal footing; as a rule one is the word taking the verbal suffixes and one functions as an apposition to the verbal subject or to the object, or as the object of the constructed word.

We look here away from the large number of words that are only formally double.

E. g., *agu ruạrket'koae.* he brought them back, *añjọm rọṛkedeañ*, I heard him say; *ñẹl janamkedeañ*; I saw him born (i. e. lived at the time of his birth); *ḍaṭa ḍhil ñũrentaea*, his teeth beeing loose came out; *lại tiok'aeme*, let him also know; *ñẹl ạgukedeañ*, I brought having seen him (i. e. I went and brought word back), *pạiye kọe ạguket'koa*, he asked them (people) for measures and brought these; *pạiye kọe ạguket'a*, he asked for and brought some measures.

177. Among these double words there are a few of constant occurrence that should be specially noted, viz. *dara*, *tora*, *baṛa*, *gọt'* and *họt'*.

(*a*) *Dara* and *tora* mean 'along with', the first being used in connection with verbs denoting coming, the second with words denoting going away from the standpoint of the subject.

E. g., *ạgu darakom*, bring them along with you; *ñẹl torakom*, look them up on your way going.

(*b*) *Baṛa* is never used alone; it always follows the principal word. The addition of *baṛa* conveys the meaning of being engaged in, occupied with or repeatedly doing what the principal word denotes. In the plural it may mean, that the act was done at separate times, one after the other, by the plural subject. *Baṛa* often conveys a side-meaning of desultorily, leisurely or even inefficiently doing what the principal word denotes.

E. g., *jom baṛaket'ako*, they are done eating; *hec' baṛayenako*, they came (one after the other); *roṛ baṛayet'ako*, people are saying; *noakoreye dãṛã baṛae kana*, he is wandering about in these parts; *gạchiye ńańam babṛa kana*, he is trying to get paddy seedlings.

(c) *Gọt'* and *hoṭ'* (with side-forms *gol* and *hol*) added to the verbal base convey the meaning that the act referred to is done quickly, without delay or suddenly.

E. g., *lại hodme*, tell it quickly; *hec' godok'me*, come quickly; *ạgu hoṭ'ket'koae*, he brought them quickly; *ńel goṭ'kedeae*, he suddenly caught sight of him; or, he saw him off, said good-by to him.

178. A number of Santal verbs are constructed impersonally, i. e. the logical subject is treated as the object of the verb and shown (when animate) by a pers. pr. infix. Verbs that denote what is felt, the effect of an external, not fixed or demonstrated cause, are constructed in this way, also some other words referring to will or occurrence. This construction naturally only occurs in the Active voice.

Many of the words that are constructed impersonally as mentioned may also be constructed with a subject, especially when the agent is known; in the Medium or the Passive the regular construction is used, generally with a somewhat different meaning.

E. g., *tetañede kana*, he is feeling thirst; *rẹṅgẹc'kedea*, he felt hungry (but *rẹṅgẹc'enae*, he became poor); *hasokidiña*, I felt pain; *sebelede kana*, he likes it, it tastes him well; *sanakedea*, he wished, felt a desire for.

Ạuriyea, he is not come as yet; *ạuriataea*, he is not ready as yet; *bañatae kana*, he is quite unwilling; *bañ ạuatae kana*, she does not care a bit (a women's expression).

Darako kana, they are coming; *darae hapta*, the coming week; *nonkan din darawa*, such days will come.

179. The Santal verb is regular; we have no so-called irregular verbs. On the other hand the language has a few words that on account of their meaning are only found in one form (or tense). These are, besides the auxiliary *kan* and *tahẹ̄kan* (already dealt with), three, viz. *dukạn*, *menak'* and *bạnuk'*.

(*a*) *Dukạn* means 'went' (presupposing return). *Haṭtele dukạna*, we went to the market place (but are back now).

(*b*) *Menak'* and *bạnuk'* are constructed like impersonal verbs with the logical subject as an infixed pers. pr. (when animate, otherwise nothing).

As the forms of the singular are somewhat irregular, the full forms are given here below.

Menak', exist (with a parallel form *henak'*).

Sing.	1st pers. anim.		*menaña* (*menạña*, *minạña*). I am, exist.
,,	2nd ,,	,,	*menama* or *menak'mea*. Thou art, existeth.
,,	3rd ,,	,,	*menaea*. He, she is, exists.
,,	,, ,,	inanim.	*menak'a*. It is, exists.

Dual 1st p. incl. anim. *menak'laṅa.* I and thou, we two are.
„ „ p. excl. „ *menak'liṅa.* I and he (she), we two are.
„ 2nd p. „ *menak'bena.* you two are.
„ 3rd p. „ *menak'kina.* They two are.

Plur. 1st p. incl. „ *menak'boa* (*menak'bona*). I and you, we are.
„ 1st p. excl. „ *menak'lea.* I and they, we are.
„ 2nd p. „ *meaak'pea.* you are.
„ 3rd p. „ *menak'koa.* They are.

With inanimate subject there is only one form *menak'a,* the base *menak'* + the finite *a. Henak'* is comparatively rare, apparently being used by preference by certain individuals. Except for the initial sound it does not in any way differ from *menak'*.

Bạnuk', not exist, not be.

Sing. 1st pers. animate *bạnugiṅa.* I am not.
„ 2nd „ „ *bạnuk'mea.* Thou art not.
„ 3rd „ „ *bạnugic'a.* He is not.
„ „ „ inanim. *bạnuk'a.* It is not.

Dual. 1st pers. incl. anim. *bạnuk'laṅa.* I and thou, we two are not.
„ 1st „ excl. „ *bạnuk'liṅa.* I and he (she), we two are not.
„ 2nd „ „ *bạnuk'bena.* You two are not.
„ 3rd „ „ *bạnuk'kina.* They two are not.

Plur. 1st „ incl. anim. *bạnuk'boa* (*bạnuk'bona*). We, I and you are not.
„ 1st „ excl. „ *bạnuk'lea.* We, I and they are
„ 2nd „ „ *bạnuk'pea.* You are not.
„ 3rd „ „ *bạnuk'koa.* They are not.

180. These verbs cannot, properly speaking, be said to belong to any tense. They denote existence or presence, and non-existence or non-presence. If a Future or a Past is wanted, other words have to be used.

Tables of the Verbal Suffixes

181. In the following tables the suffixes of the Santal verb are shown.

Note : (+ anim. obj. infix) or (+ anim. or inanim. obj. infix) in parenthesis is intended to show the place of the obj. infix when such has to be used. Except in certain tenses of the form with indirect object and of the Intentional form there is no inanimate obj. infix. Intransitive verbs naturally have no obj. infix.

The optional possessive infix always follows the object infix, if any such is used. It may come immediately after the obj. infix or after *kan* or after *tahẽkan* in tenses where these occur. When no object infix has to be used the possessive infix may (but must not) stand where the obj. infix should have been.

Table I. The General Form of the Verb with direct object.

Tense		Active	Medium and Passive
Indeterminate and Future	Base	(+anim. obj. infix)	*ok'* (- *k'*)
Indefinite Present	,,	*et'* (+anim. obj. infix)	*ok'* (- *k'*) *kan*
Definite Present	,,	*et'* (+anim. obj. infix) *kan*	
Indefinite Imperfect	,,	*et'* (+anim. obj. infix) *tahẽkan*	*ok'* (- *k'*) *kan tahẽkan*
Definite Imperfect	,,	*et'* (+anim. obj. infix) *kan tahẽkan*	
Simple Past	,,	*ket'* (+anim. obj. infix)	*en*
Anterior Past	,,	*let'* (+anim. obj. infix)	*len*
Anterior Pluperfect	,,	*let'* (+anim. obj. infix) *tahẽkan*	*len tahẽkan*
Accidental Past	,,	—	*ken*
Optative	,,	*ke* (+anim. obj. infix)	*kok'*
Anterior	,,	*le* (+anim. obj. infiix)	*len*

Table II. The General Form of the Verb with indirect object.

Tense		Active	Medium
Indeterminate and Future	Base	*a* (+anim. or inanim. obj. infix)	*joṅ*
Indefinite Present	—	—	—
Definite Present	,,	*a* (+anim. or inanim. obj. infix) *kan*	*joṅ kan*
Indefinite Imperfect	—	—	—
Definite Imperfect	,,	*a* (+anim. or inanim. obj. infix) *kan tahẽkan*	*joṅ kan tahẽkan*
Simple Past	,,	*at'* (+anim. obj. infix)	*an*
Anterior Past	—	—	—
Anterior Pluperfect	,,	*at'* (+anim. obj. infix) *tahẽkan*	*an tahẽkan*
Accidental Past	—	—	—
Optative	,,	*ke* (+anim. obj. infix)	*kok'*
Anterior	,,	*le* (+anim. obj. infix)	*len*

Table III. The Intentional Form of the Verb.

Tense		Active	Medium and Passive	Indirect Medium (Reflexive)
Indeterminate and Future	Base	*ka*(+anim. or inanimate object infix)	*kok'*	*kok'*
Definite Present	,,	*ka*(+anim. or inanim. obj. infix) *kan*	*kok' kan*	*kok' kan*
Definite Imperfect	,,	*ka*(+anim. or inanim. obj. infix) *kan tahẽkan*	*kok' kan tahẽkan*	*kok kan tahẽkan*
Simple Past	,,	*kat'* (+anim. obj. infix)	*kan*	—
Anterior Past	,,	*lak'*	—	—
Anterior Pluperfect	,,	*kat'* (+anim. obj. infix) *tahẽkan*	—	—
Perfect with direct object	,,	*akat'* (+anim. obj. infix)	*akan*	—
,, with indirect obj.	,,	*akawat'* (+anim. obj. infix)	—	*akawan*
Pluperfect with direct obj.	,,	*akat'* (+anim. obj. infix) *tahẽkan*	*akan tahẽkan*	—
,, with indirect obj.	,,	*akawat'* (+anim. obj. infix) *tahẽkan*	—	*akawan tahẽkan*

Conjunctions, Conjunctional Adverbs, Particles and Interjections.

Copulatives.

182. (*a*) *Ar*, and also, further, more.

Apattẹt' ar gidrạko, the father and his children; *aṅak' ar poṇḍ*, red and white; *holae hẹc'ena ar gapae calak'a*, he came yesterday and will go to-morrow; *ar ẹmok'me*, give more.

(*b*) - *hõ* (or *hõ*), also, even, too. A postpositional particle.

Onko hõñ ṅẹlket'koa, I saw also them; *ẹnre hõe calaoena*, in spite of this he went.

(*c*) - *hõ* - *hõ*, both - and, as well - as also.

Iñ hõ am hõ, both you and I; *dal hõko dalkedea, jẹret' hõko jeret'kedea*, they both beat him and set fire to his house.

Temporal conjunctions.

183. (*a*) *Adọ*, and, so, then, further, moreover, more. Used to connect sentences, also adverbially; it is often combined with *khange*.

Adọ khange onka hudis baṛakate atoren họṛ ṭhen khon barea pạiye kọe ạguket'a; adọ onako pẹnẹ pạiye khadleket'a; khange adọe jolak' kana are ghanṭayet'a, thereupon having thought over this he asked the village people for three pai-measures and brought these; so he put all three pai-measures into the cooking pot; thereupon he makes a fire and stirs.

(*b*) *Khan* and *khange* (with parallel forms *khac'* and *khac'ge*), then, thereupon. *Khan* is really a postposition (see para 170). It is often used added to a demonstrative adverb or element. When used as a conjunction, a previous statement or condition is implied.

Uniye hec'enkhan ẹṇḍẹkhan (or, *tọbẹkhan*) *ale dọle chuṭiyena*, when he came we became free, were released ; *ma ẹṇḍẹkhan jọmme*, then please take your food ; *khangeko calaoena*, so they went.

(*c*) *Ẹnkhan, ẹnkhac', ẹnkhante*, and *ẹnkhac'te*, then, in that case, then only, after that. It is temporal, but also refers to the *conditio sine qua non* for an action.

Hẹrẹle jọmlege, ẹnkhante oṛak' hoṛtẹt' dọe jọmgea, when the man has first eaten, then only the wife will eat.

(*d*) *Jãhãtisre*, whenever ; *jãhãtinre*, whenever (during day or night), at any hour. Really indefinite pronominal adverbs, but frequently used as conjunctions.

184. *Ạuri* has been called a temporal conjunction ; this is not correct. It is mentioned here, because beginners make so many mistakes using it. We conveniently translate it 'not yet' with a following past tense. In Santali the word is used in many ways, as a noun, an adjective, a verb (constructed impersonally, with the subject as object infix) and as an adverb. It means 'delay', 'later', 'out of season', 'afterwards'. *Ạuriko hijuk'a*, they will come delayed, later (*ạuriko hẹc' akana*, is a fearful howler). *Ạuri* is always constructed with the Future of the verb.

Santali makes use of this *ạuri* followed by a verb in the Future and one of the postpositions *dhạbic'* (with parallel forms *hạbic', dhạric'* and *hạric'*), *re* and *te* (*ge*) to express a subordinate clause with the conjunction 'until' or 'before'.

Auriń emam dhabic', until I give you; *auriye calak're*, before he goes; *cando auriye hasurok'tege*, before the sun sets.

Disjunctives.

185. *Se*, or. Often used added to a verb or a negation (*ba*), corresponding to 'or how', 'is it not so ?'

Hor se deko, a Santal or a Deko; *jinisem emok'a se takam halawańa*, will you give goods (here mustard seed) or will you pay me the money ?

186. (*a*) *Bańdo*, whether. Introduces an indirect question; the verb of the sentence introduced by *bańdo* does not take the finite *a*.

Nonde khon bańdo ńel ńamok', (I wonder) whether it may be seen from here; *bań badaea, bańdoe calaoen*, I do not know, whether he has gone.

(*b*) *Bańdo* - *bańdo*, whether - or.

Bańdo hor bańdo bonga, whether man or spirit; *bańdoe calaoen, bańdo orak're menae, ohoń men darelea*, whether he is gone or he is at home, I am unable to say.

(*c*) - *hõ ba* (*ń*), also not, nor, not - either, not even.*

\- *hõ ba*(*ń*) - *hõ ba*(*ń*), neither - nor.

See para 182 (b) and (c). These disjunctive particles ar used both with single words and with compounds, but not with full sentences.

Am hõ bań, not you either, not even you; *ror hõ bań ror akat'a, ruhet' hõ bań ruhet' akadea*, I have neither spoken, nor have I scolded him.

* - *hõ ba*(*ń*) added to an interrogative pronoun or adverb is used to make negative demonstrative pronouns and adverbs, the interrogative being lost to the sense. *Cet' hõ bań*, nothing; *okare hõ bań*, nowhere; *okalekate hõ bań*, in no way at all.

187. (*a*) *Hoe - hoe*, either - or. Mostly used with sentences, about alternatives. Always prefixed.

Hoe mit' hor thene jamarok', *hoe mit' hore kurudae*, he will either hold to one, or he will hate one.

(*b*) *Ek - ek*, *ek do - ek do*, either - or. About alternatives; always prefixed the word or the sentence to which it is attached.

Ek doe hundar kana, *ek doe tarup' kana*, it is either a wolf or it is a leopard; *gai eke aguye*, *eke tahẽ ocoae*, he will either bring the cow or he will let it remain.

(*c*) - *co(ṅ)* - *co(ṅ)*, either - or;

- *co(ṅ)* - *baṅ co(ṅ)*, whether - or not.

The particle *co(ṅ)* expresses uncertainty (it may also be used as an affirmative particle, see below para 195 (c)). When doubled it is used to express the subjective doubt as to which of two alternatives. *Coṅ* is always postpositional.

Okoe badae coṅ, *hẽ coṅ baṅ coṅ*, who knows? it may be true or it may not; *horo coṅ jondra coko agu akat'a*, they have brought either paddy or Indian corn (I do not know which); *lai coe baṅ coṅ*, (one cannot say) whether he will tell or not.

Adversatives.

188. (*a*) *Menkhan*, but (lit. 'if said' or 'when saying (so)'). Used as here mentioned it is always prefixed; it may also be used as a postposition in conditional sentences. *Menkhan*, but, may be used both in connection with single words and with full sentences.

Joto hoṛe lạị akawat'koa, mẹnkhan iń do bań, he has told all, but not me; *kulạiyiń ńẹlledea, mẹnkhan bań sap' daṛeadea*, I saw the hare, but was unable to catch it.

(*b*) ***Mẹnẹk*** (*menek*), but, however. Used like *mẹnkhan*, but less frequently. It is also used in the meaning of 'as for that', 'however'.

Calak'e mẹnlak'a, mẹnẹk bae sẹnlena, he intended to go, but did not; *kạphariạu jokhẹc' menek bań tahẽkana*, I was not, however, present at the time of the quarrel.

(*c*) ***Bickom***, rather, but rather, on the contrary, preferably.

Uni bańkate bickom nuigeń hataoea, I will rather take this one than that one; *nitok' do bickom bań calak'a, tayomteń calak'a*, I prefer not to go now, I shall go later on.

(*d*) ***Boroń***, *boroń co(ń)*, *bor co(ń)*, rather, preferably. *Bor coń* is rare. Used very much like *bickom*.

Hoṛ ḍher do bako sẹnlena, boroń deko baṛtigeko tahẽkana, many Santals had not gone there, rather there were more Dekos; *iń do bań calak'a, boroń coń iń bodol amge calak'me*, I shall not go, you better go in my place.

(*e*) ***Bańkhan***, *bańkhac'*, if not, or else, otherwise, naturally, of course.

Onka do alom roṛa, bańkhanlań dalmea, don't speak in this way, else I shall thrash you; *jom bańkhane cekaea?* lit. eating if not what will he do? i. e. of course he will eat; *ẹm akawadeam? bańkhac' do*, have you given it to him? Of course I have.

(*f*) ***Ẹn hõ***, *ẹnre hõ*, even then, yet, still, nevertheless.

Manakedeaṅ, ẹn hõe calaoena, I forbade (or, warned) him, still he went; *jãhãtinạk'em emaere hõ, ẹnre hõ bae tirpitok' kana*, however much you give him, still he is not satisfied.

Causals.

189. *Ẹnte*, because, for, as. Used as an adverb postpositionally it may be translated: by all means, all right, of course, why, then. When used as a conjunction the sentence introduced by *ẹnte* gives the cause or reason of the previous statement.

Alom bọtọrok'a, ẹnte iṅ menaṅa, don't be afraid, for I am here; *uni ẹnteye rọṛ akat'a*, why, he has said so.

In certain parts of the country educated Santals now frequently use *cedak' je* in stead of *ẹnte*. It is a rendering of a Hindi expression.

Conclusives.

190. (*a*) *Onate*, by that (cause or means), for that reason, therefore, thereby, so that. Used as a conjunction to state the result of a previous statement, to which *onate* refers. The finite *a* may be left out.

Katha akawat'koale, onateko hẹc' gọdọk'a nãhãk', we have sent them word, so they will come here presently; *galmaraoat'koae, onateko bujhạuket'*, he spoke to them, so they understood.

(*b*) *Ona iạte, ona tẹrọṅ, ona karọnte*, on account of that, for that reason, therefore. All these are used in the same way, recapitulating a previous statement that gives the reason for what follows. In stead of *ona* (the most commonly used) any other demonstrative may be employed, when suitable or wanted.

Ruak' kan tahẹkanań, ona tẹroṅ (or - *iate*, or *karonte*) *bań hẹc'lena*, I was ill, therefore I did not come.

Eṇḍẹkhan (- *khac'*), *tobẹkhan* (- *khac'*), then, thereupon, in that case.

Represents the previous statement, giving the temporal precedence and condition for what follows.

Eṇḍẹkhan amge calak'tabonme, so then you please go for us ; *tobẹkhane dalkedea*, thereupon he struck him.

(*d*) The demonstrative adverb *eṇḍẹ* is used with one or the other of a number of postpositions to convey the meaning of 'then', 'in that case', the sense of locality in *eṇḍẹ* having become changed into the idea of temporal condition. Besides above mentioned *eṇḍekhan* we have :

eṇḍẹ anań (- *anẹc'*, - *ena*, - *enań*, - *ẹnẹc'*, - *ẹroń*, - *rẹsẹt'*, - *bapo*, - *moto*, - *nũhĩ*), then only ;

eṇḍẹre (- *ma*, - *sẹ*), there, then, in that case, then only ; (with past tense) why, I thought.

eṇḍẹre anań (- *anẹc'*, etc. as with *eṇḍẹ*), then only.

eṇḍẹte, in that case, then, thereupon ; why.

eṇḍẹte anań (- *anẹc'*, etc. as above), then only.

eṇḍẹrege (- *tege*), (when followed by Future) then ; (when followed by past tense) why, I have heard.

As is seen, all above mentioned are really adverbs.

(*e*) Descriptive sentences may be introduced by *cet' leka, cet' lekate, oka leka* and *oka lekate*, how, in what way.

Conjunctives.

191. Besides those mentioned under Copulatives (- *hõ* - *hõ*)

ẹkẹn - dọ baṅ, mẹnkhan - hǫ̃, not only, but also;
- eskar dọ baṅ, mẹnkhan - hǫ̃, not - alone, but also.
In stead of *mẹnkhan - hǫ̃* simply *ge* may be used. In stead of *baṅ*, when needed, *alo* is used.

Ẹkẹn gidrạko dọ baṅ (or *gidrạko eskar dọ baṅ*), *mẹnkhan sẽrã hoṛ hǫ̃*, not only the children, but also the grown up people; *ẹkẹn am* (or *am eskar*) *dọ alo, jọtọkoge hijuk'pe*, not only you (you alone), come all of you.

Conditionals.

192. The postposition *khan* is added to the protasis; *ẹnḍẹkhan* or *tọbẹkhan*, recapitulating the condition of the protasis, introduces the apodosis. See above para 190 (c).

Khạjuk, provided, if only. Used to introduce the condition sine qua non for the statement of the apodosis. The verb is always without the finite *a*; the negation used in connection with *khạjuk* is *alo*.

Gapaṅ calak'a, khạjuk aloe dag, I shall go tomorrow, provided it does not rain.

Judi, if, recently borrowed, is used to introduce the protasis.

Comparatives.

193. The use of *khon* to form comparatives has been mentioned (see para 36).

To compare the language has the postposition *leka*; as a postposition added to a word or a sentence, it serves as a conjunction equal to 'like' or 'as'. Added to the interrogative pronouns *cet'* and *oka*, we get *cet' leka* and *oka leka*, that are frequently used as conjunctions, always placed in front of the word or the sentence to which they refer; they may be taken up in a following *onka leka* or similar word. By adding the instrumental *te* the words become more descriptive. *Re* may also be added.

Disạime, cet' leka tahẹ̃kantam, remember, how you had it; *uduk'aeme, cet' lekateye kạmi,* show him, how he is to work; *cet' leka am iñ hǫ̃ onka lekage,* as you so also I; *lạime, oka lekatem ạsulok' kan,* tell, in what way you are supporting yourself.

Finals.

194. To introduce final clauses the language makes use of *jãhã lekate,* and *jẹmọn* (this last word borrowed in fairly recent times from Bengali), both corresponding to 'in order that', 'that', or similar expressions.

Lạiakom, jãhãlekate (or *jẹmọn*) *aloko sorok',* tell them that they must not go near.

Subservient particles.

195. The language has a few particles that serve to draw attention to, to emphasize or to express doubt or mental reservation. They are always suffixed to a word; they have no separate existence; they may get the stress. They are:

(*a*) *ge,* a generally untranslatable particle, emphasizing the word to which it is added; *ge* may be added to single words, to suffixes and to postpositions If translated, it may be 'certainly', 'really', or something similar.

Ac'geye rọṛ akat'a, he has said it himself; *rọṛge bae rọṛet',* he does not speak at all; *sạrige,* really, truly; *nui kangeae naṭer guru dọ,* this one is the mischief-maker; *hẹc'engeae,* he has really come; *uniye hẹc'enkhange,* when he had come.

(*b*) *dọ,* as for, with reference to, concerning. Generally not translated. *Dọ* draws attention to; it is very frequently used as a suffix to the subject, sometimes also to the object.

Iñ dọ bañ, amge, not I, but you; *nitok' dọ mit' serma hoyena,* now it is one year since (it happened); *noko dọ ale leka dọ bako cọlọna,* as for these they do not behave like us; *adọm lebṛa họṛ dọ sẹnge bako sẹnok'a ọṇḍẹ dọ,* some covetous people do not go there at all; *bana dọko gọc'kedea, khikṛi dọko phaskaokedea,* they killed they bear, but the fox they lost.

(c) *cọ(ñ),* perhaps; who knows; why.

Cọñ has been mentioned under the disjunctive conjunctions (see para 18). It is used in a double way, to express subjective doubt, and also to meet the doubt of another person, in which case it becomes an affirmative particle. When attached to the verb, the finite *a* is not used.

Ọkọe cọko hẹc'en, somebody or other (who knows who) have come; *ac' cọe bae akat',* why, he has himself put it aside; *nũk'ũi cọñ,* why, here he is; *nọ̃k'ọ̃e cọñ,* why, here it is.

(*d*) - *tẹt'* is a particle suffixed to emphasize, especially the identity.

Noatẹt', this very; *ac'tẹt',* he himself; *nũk'ũi kombṛotẹt',* this one is the very, real thief; *ḍạrtẹt'ko ạguime, daretẹt' ikạkak'me,* bring the branches, let the tree itself be; *kạmitẹt'reñ tebak'kedea,* I cought him in the very act; *sạriak'tẹt',* the very truth.

(*e*) *tǫ, thǫ, thǫr,* surely, you know. Not generally translatable.

Hẽ thǫ, yes, that's it; *khange thǫ,* so thereupon; *amren kangeae tǫ,* he is thine to be sure; *ma ńũime tǫ,* drink then.

Affirmative particles.

196. (*a*) *Hẽ,* yes.

Hẹc'enae? *Hẽ, hẹc'enae,* has he come? yes, he has; *hẽ sạrige,* yes, truly; *hẽ ẹnte,* yes, of course; *hẽge cǫń,* yes likely, may be; *hẽ jạnic',* yes, probably; *hẽket'-ae,* he said yes, he agreed.

(*b*) *Hẽk',* a side form to *hẽ,* more especially used as a verb.

(*c*) *Hã,* a sideform to *hẽ* (pure Hindi, rarely used).

(*d*) *Hẽ hũ* is not used as a particle, but as a verb in the sense of assenting to.

(*e*) *Hạị, hǫị,* yes, quite so, just so; will you, won't you, do.

Both used partly as an affirmative particle, partly as an interjection.

Hijuk'me! hạị (or *hǫị*), *calak' kanań,* come! yes, I am on my way; *alom lạia hạị,* don't tell please; *dẹn, iń hǫ̃ bape imańa?* *hǫị, emamalań,* please, will you not give me also? Just so, we two shall give you (i. e. certainly not).

Particles of negation.

197. (*a*) *Ba, bań,* no, not.

Ba(ń) is the simple assertive negation. Besides it is used in certain connections enclitically added to other words, conveying the meaning of 'why', 'well', etc. Prefixed another word it corresponds to *un* - or *in* -.

When used as an assertive negation a verb with the suffix of the Simple Past cannot be used; the suffixes of the Anterior Past (or any other tense) may be used.

Calaoenae? Baṅ, bae sẹn akana, has he gone? No, he has not; *uni sọṅgẹtekhan dọ hẹge, baṅkhan baṅtẹl'ge,* if together with him, I am willing; otherwise absolutely not; *bae hẹc'ena mẹnkhan,* if he does not come (note tense suffix; there is no assertive negation); *baṅ sẹ, onka dọ baṅ kana,* no, it is not so; *okor ba,* no, don't you see, nowhere here; *cet' baṅ sẹ, ọhọm pạtiạulena,* you have no idea how it was, you would never believe it; *baṅ gujuk' ọt,* land on which crops will not die; *baṅ ṅẹlogok'ak',* what is invisible.

(*b*) *Ọhọ,* no, not, not at all, certainly not.

Ọhọ is emphatic, assuring. When connected with a verb, this generally has the suffix of the Anterior, but it may also be in the Future. The first conveys a general negation, the second refers to the special case mentioned.

Ọhọe hẹẹlena, he will certainly not come; *ọhọṅ mẹnlea,* I am unable to say; *ọhọtẹt'geṅ ẹmlekoa,* I am absolutely unwilling to give them; *ọhọe gujuk'a,* he will surely not die (this time); *ọhọ tọko jãhã cekamea,* they will surely not do anything to you.

(*c*) *Alo,* no, don't.

Alo is a prohibitive particle, whether it be an order or a wish. The verb following is always in the Future, not in the Imperative. It is the negation used in final clauses, and in conditional clauses with a condition sine qua non.

Alom rọṛa, don't speak; *alotẹt'gem ẹmok'a,* don't give under any circumstances; *bes leka tọlme, jẹmọn alo raṛak',* tie it well, so it may not be loosened;

aloń sẹnlenkhan uni tuluc' dọ ọhọń ńẹpẹllena, if I had not gone, I should not have met him.

Interjections.

198. Santali has a very large assortment of interjections to call attention, to warn, threaten or encourage, to express admiration, surprise, joy, grief, sorrow, pain, or any kind of feeling. Most of these are used by all, others only by men or only by women, some only to men, others only to women.

Most of them are prefixed, some are added to another word.

To call attention.

199. *E*, o, oh, hey; *ẹa, ẹya, ea,* listen, look here (used only to younger or inferior males; also in rebuking).

Ei, look here, listen, hallo (familiar, used between equals, never to superiors).

E̱ họ, oh, I say, hallo, listen (used by men to all).

E̱ hǫ, oh, I say, listen (equal to *ẹ họ,* but used by women to women).

Iạ, iạ họ, I say.

-họ, oh, listen, I say, you there. Always added to another word or interjection; used by men calling upon other men.

-hǫ, listen, I say. Equal to *-họ,* but used by women to women.

Henda, listen, look here, hey, I say. Used to call attention, especially also in questioning.

-ya, you boy, young man, you chap, you fellow. Always suffixed to a preceding word or another interjection. Used by all to males younger than oneself.

-na, you girl. Used like *-ya*, but only to females younger than the speaker.

-yọi, *-nọi*, hallo there, look out there, have a care. Used like *-ya* and *-na* respectively, but generally to a number; it often conveys a warning.

Hui, *hui hui*, get off, away (used at night or in forest thickets to warn any one possibly present, but not seen.

-rẹ, oh you, sirrah. Interjection of calling or of intensification; always suffixed.

Ek̈, *ẹk̈*, er, ah, look. Also used as an expletive in enumerations.

Ẹk ẹk̈ ẹk̈, oh.

Affirmative and negative.

200. *Hại*, *hại hại*, *họi*, *hoi họi*, yes, yes yes.
Ọi, *ọi ọi*, yes, what is it, take care.
Ā, how, what is it, eh.
Ẹ̄hẹ̄k̈ ẹ̄hẹ̄k̈, *ẹ̄hẹ̄k̈*, *ōhōk̈*, *ūhūk̈*, no, not so, not at all, nothing of the kind.

Warning or remonstrating.

201. *Ạikạ*, *ạikhạ*, mind, I warn you, but, only, on the understanding.

Ią ạikạ, I say, but remember.

Hāhā, *hāhāk̈*, take care, beware, stop, hold, don't.

Ahak̈, don't, take care, hold, stop.

Aha, *aha aha*, alas, it's a pity.

Ahaha, *aha haha*, don't, stop, hands off.

Mẹn, mind, take care, beware, look out.

Ẹhẹ, *ẹhẹ ẹhẹ*, *ẹhẹge*, *ẹhẹrẹ*, hey there, be careful, keep off there, hist.

Oho, take care.

The words for father and mother with or without a prefixed *ẹ* and with or without a suffixed *rẹ* are used as exclamations to express surprise, astonishment, annoyance, pain or even anger. *Babarẹ*, *ẹ baba*, *baba gọ*, *ayọ*, *ayọgọ*, *ayoge*, *ayogo*.

Ạige, *ạiyo*, hallo, dear me, what.

Ạijo, *ạjjo*, *ajjo*, what, is it possible, strange.

To express surprise.

202. *Durrẹ*, *durẹ*, hallo, strange.

Ẹh, *ẹh ẹh*, *ẹhrẹ*, *eh*, *eh eh*, *ehre*, o, what, indeed, really, my, o dear.

To express annoyance, concern and pain.

203. *Eh*, oh, o my, dear me.

Ehe hehe he, *eh hehe hehe*, o dear dear.

Ẹh ẹhẹ, *ẹhẹ hẹ*, *ẹhẹ hẹhẹ*, oh, dear me, alas.

Oh ho, *ohre*, *oh hoho ho*, alas, dear me, oh.

Ọh, *ọh ọh*, *ọh ọhọ*, oh, dear me, alas, what a pity.

Uh, *uhre*, alas, dear me oh.

Uhu, *uhu uhu*, *u huhu*, *u huhu huhu*, *uh huhuhu*, alas, oh, dear.

I, *ih*, *ih ih*, oh, dear, me, fie.

Is, *is is*, oh, dear me, get away, fie.

Aege, hallo, dear me, oh, o dear.

Ạigu, oh, o dear, dear me.

Ạu, *ạu ạu*, oh, ah, o dear.

Ọ, oh, well, alas.

Họ, well, oh.

O hae, *ọ hae hae*, oh, dear me, alas, to think! (Used by women to express surprise, astonishment, regret, sorrow, pain).

To express pain, sorrow, pity.

204. *Hae, hae hae, haere, haere hae, haere haere*, oh, alas, o dear, woe (especially also used at lamentations, and may give expression to the deepest grief).

Jare jare, alas, woe (used by women, especially in lamentation).

Durrę, durę, durhạk̇, dur kharak̇, dhurhạk̇, dhur karak̇, dur karahak̇, oh, hallo, alas, woe is me, strange, fie.

Dir, dirre, dirhak̇, dir karak̇, dhir, dhirre, dhirhak̇, oh, hallo, alas.

Mor, morhak̇, morre, mor jala, oh, alas, what a pity.

Dhiṭ, dhiṭhak̇, dhuṭ, dhuṭhak̇, oh, fie.

To express pleasure and joy.

205. *Ah, ah ah, aha, a haha, a haha haha*, oh, ah, how pleasent.

Hạlạ, hạlạre, bravo, well done, hurrah.

Bah, bah bah, bahwarę, baoha baohare, bravo, well done, excellent.

Exhortative particles.

206. *Do*, do, please.

Dę, dęn, do, please, let us, give.

Dini, dinkin, dęnko, give him (the two, those).

-sę, do, please. Always postpositional.

Ma, do, please, let them.

Mę, do, come along, get.

Dela, delaṅ, delabo(n), delalaṅ, delọi, come, come along.

mela, melaṅ, melalaṅ, melabo(n), melọi, do, come, come along.

THE END.